PROFESSIONAL COACHING!

Is it Time to Hire a Coach?

Françoise Depéry | Nathalie Ducrot | Virginia Williams

PROFESSIONAL
COACHING!

Is it Time to Hire a Coach?

10 practical questions & answers to help you decide

What is professional coaching?
What can you expect? When? How? And with whom?
What is a "real" coach? How do you find one?
What is coaching and what is *not* coaching?
You hired a coach, now how do you manage the process?
And what can you expect following your coaching engagement?

With this practical guide and its many examples and testimonies, you will discover how coaching works, how to take advantage of coaching, and ultimately what it can do for you now and in the future.
Three internationally recognized professional coaches explain their craft, its possibilities, its limitations and the "know how" of coaching.
The authors offer simple, concrete and documented responses to a series of helpful questions that you ask yourself about professional coaches and coaching.

> A "must have" resource for clients and coaches to use
> before, during and after
> the entire coaching process

http://www.professional-coaching.net

Professional Coaching! Is it Time to Hire a Coach?
10 practical questions and answers to help you decide / Françoise Depéry, Nathalie Ducrot, Virginia Williams
Includes bibliographical references and multi-media files
    1.   Business & Economics, 2. Coaching and Mentoring
Illustrations by Marion Depéry and Sophie Depéry

Adapted from – "Un coach peut-il m'aider et comment?" / Françoise Depéry, Nathalie Ducrot (InterEditions 2013, Paris, France)

ISBN-10: 1482647893
ISBN-13: 978-1482647891
First printed 2013

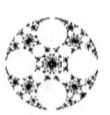

CONTENTS

HOW TO GET THE MOST
FROM THIS BOOK

Reading this book will help you...

✓ Know what kind of help you can expect from a professional coach

✓ Understand the legitimacy of the profession of coaching

✓ Get practical information about this growing profession

✓ Move away from complicated, academic theories about coaching

✓ Understand how to best take advantage of your coaching process

✓ Familiarize yourself with the possibilities and limits of coaching

✓ Be able to spot when coaching is misused or misrepresented

✓ Explain the benefits of coaching to others (including your boss)

✓ Benefit from recent independent global surveys and research about the return on investment of coaching

✓ Understand how professional coaching is an integral part of today's society

✓ Know how to get yourself in a resourceful state to achieve your goals while maintaining balance and peace of mind

---

The format of this book offers you practical questions and answers relating to professional coaching and its benefits and limitations.

FOR CLIENTS AND POTENTIAL CLIENTS: This book is the essential how-to guide to decide when, how and whom to hire as your coach, how to successfully manage the coaching process, and how to sustain your learning. With the full range of resources in this book, you are sure to find the right fit for a successful and rewarding experience whenever you want to engage a professional coach.

FOR COACHES: It is a useful resource for you to know more about what clients expect of their coach, how to progress your own coaching practices and is *the* book to offer to your clients and potential clients.

Icons used in this book

To make this book easy to read and understand, we use a variety of modes and visual styles. Throughout the book you will find icons to indicate different kinds of material. Here is a key to the icons we use.

 Represents questions for you, the reader, to ask yourself.

 Represents a coaching case study to demonstrate points made in the chapter.

 Indicates an inspiring quote for further reflection.

 Marks space for your notes, reflections and reminders.

 QR codes indicate online resources

Other useful links

To further increase the usefulness of this book and to expand your understanding around specific points, you are kindly invited to scan the QR codes and click on other links throughout the book to discover complementary video, audio, online sites and other relevant material. You will also find a list of additional resources at the end of the book. (see p.135)

INTRODUCTION

WELCOME TO THE REAL WORLD OF PROFESSIONAL COACHING!

Through a set of **10 simple and practical questions and answers,** this book enables you to understand professional coaching and help you decide if coaching could be useful for you, and if so, when, how and with whom.

We invite you to get to know some real professional coaches so that if you need one you will be able to choose with full knowledge and confidence. Professional coaches have met a validated and rigorous set of standards and qualifications. Given the proliferation of untrained self-proclaimed coaches, choosing a coach is not always straight forward.

In the media, at work, or over dinner, you might hear the words "coach" and "coaching" referring to just about anything, which creates widespread confusion. These words are obviously overused and everyone has their own understanding of them. No more advertising as hair stylists, insurance agents or financial advisers - they all pretend to be coaches! A landscape architect claims he "coaches" his clients to design the garden, the auto mechanic "coaches" his apprentice, Julie prides herself on "coaching" her cousin on her "look" and her neighbor about his mood.

Alongside this curious variety of self-declared coaches, you also find professional coaches - well trained, fully qualified, experienced and capable of providing you with reliable coaching services in many different circumstances.

Who are the authors?

We are three professional certified coaches with extensive and diverse business experience. We each hold the Professional Certified Coach (PCC) credential awarded by the International Coach Federation (ICF). Our clients are leaders, managers and business professionals, and owners of companies as well as private individuals. We are all three actively involved with ICF - globally, regionally and locally – and have led the local ICF Switzerland chapter for many years. We rigorously support our profession by bringing a clearer understanding of professional coaching, modeling professional behavior and working to improve credibility and visibility about this relatively new field for the general population, the public sector and the business marketplace.

By now you are most likely convinced that, for us, coaching is both our profession and our passion. As passionate professionals with a keen interest to demonstrate the depth and breadth of coaching, we include our personal and professional experience, client testimonials, practical information and reliable figures backed up by recent research, surveys and studies wherever possible.

Our brief bios are on page 141 and our website, LinkedIn and Twitter links are below.

For more >>
Françoise Depéry, PCC
www.deperypartner.ch
LinkedIn

For more >>
Nathalie Ducrot, PCC
www.prooptim.com
LinkedIn

For more >>
Virginia Williams, MBA, PCC
www.ventures-worldwide.com
LinkedIn | Twitter @vworldwide

What information did we consider for this book?

To get a broad view beyond our personal experiences and opinions, we consulted many recognized sources and solicited feedback from other coach colleagues and professional associations, as well as extensive online resources. In addition, we reviewed and summarized with care relevant publications, books and research papers as well as polls and surveys on the subject.

Also bear in mind that the International Coach Federation is in the best possible position to observe and document the evolution of the coaching profession globally. Each year, coach members, clients, human resources professionals and others involved in the coaching profession are invited to participate in various surveys. In recent years, ICF mandated PricewaterhouseCoopers, the globally recognized multinational professional services firm, through its International Survey Unit (ISU), to conduct global surveys to document the current state of the world of professional coaching.

Wherever possible, we have chosen to provide figures relating to results from participants globally. In some cases where significant variations occur, we also provide regional figures.

For more >>
PricewaterhouseCoopers surveys and studies
www.professional-coaching.net

1
WHAT IS A PROFESSIONAL COACH?

WHAT ARE THE ROOTS OF COACHING?

Professional coaching began around the mid 1980's in the United States and has roots dating earlier in other forms. In 1995, a professional association emerged: the International Coach Federation (ICF). Currently, ICF is present in 120 countries and has more than 22,000 members, all of whom have completed coach-specific training. The **ICF is the leading global professional coaching organization** dedicated to advancing the coaching profession by setting high standards, providing independent certification, and building a worldwide network of credentialed coaches. As a pioneer of professional coach associations, ICF leads the profession with a code of ethics and an accreditation process to enable any client to know the level of training and experience of the coach.

Today, three coaching organizations - International Coach Federation (ICF), European Mentoring & Coaching Council (EMCC) and Association for Coaching (AC) - have teamed up to create the Global Coaching and Mentoring Alliance (GCMA) (ICF, 2011). Together these three associations have established goals and initiatives and have developed a commonly-agreed code of conduct for all members.

The profession is advancing rapidly, growing exponentially, and becoming more visible to the general public. As an example of recent activity in Europe, where the coaching market is less developed than it is in the USA, in 2011 the ICF and EMCC submitted a Code of Conduct for Coaching and Mentoring to the European Commission. This Professional Charter was accepted and published in the Self- and Co-Regulation database which is co-managed by the Single Market Observatory (SMO) and the European Economic and Social Committee (EESC). The Charter establishes a set of guidelines whose primary goals are to establish a benchmark for ethics and good practice in coaching, to inform clients, and to promote public confidence in coaching and mentoring as a process for professional and personal development.

The Professional Charter requires coaches and mentors to abide explicitly by a Code of Ethics containing minimum standards of ethics and professional behavior. It further requires that professional organizations, associations and federations include a commitment to these guidelines as a condition of individual membership. Finally, the Professional Charter requires that professional organizations have in place a procedure to monitor and deal with cases of alleged breach of the Charter. This publicly accessible database includes codes of conduct for other professions such as the Council of Bar and Law Societies and the European Association for Psychotherapy. (ICF, 2011)

The word "coach" is derived from Old French "coche" or "kocsi" in Hungarian. The coachman's job is to drive passengers safely from *where they are* to *where they want to go*. This is a fitting metaphor for the role of the professional coach. If you take a stagecoach, or to update the image, a taxi, you choose your destination and the driver ensures the safety of your route. Thanks to the talent and skills of the driver, the passenger is able to admire the scenery along the way and arrive at their desired destination. As an extension of this metaphor, the core focus of coaching is to accompany coachees on their life journey: to realize their full potential, to develop personally and professionally, and to enjoy the process. Coaching is all of this and more.

WHO IS A COACH AND WHO IS NOT?

You would not go to a doctor who is not specifically trained and certified! You trust that the doctor has been properly trained and has the legal right to practice. For coaches, it is more complicated because this profession is still in its early stages and it will take some time before appropriate laws and regulations are universally in place.

In the meantime, you have probably met or know people who tell you they are coaches yet the description of their activities varies widely. We want to emphasize that coaching is a specialized profession with its own benefits and limits.

To begin with, we would like to make it clear what a coach is not. When someone's exclusive function is to explain, propose, teach, advise, counsel, or train, then he or she is engaging, respectively, as consultant, teacher, counselor, trainer or other service provider. He or she may be empathetic and even helpful but not necessarily a professional coach! We come across many self-proclaimed "coaches" who have a few days of training in personal development or a weekend coaching course but cannot seriously claim to be qualified coaches, despite the words on their freshly printed cards.

COACHING IS A COMPLETELY INDEPENDENT PROFESSION!

Perhaps you have yourself experienced someone telling you that she or he is a coach and you do not really know what that means! No wonder there is confusion when the word is used so loosely! You need more details about the person's coaching expertise, training and experience.

To respond to this need, we offer you this set of **ten practical questions and answers** to provide insight into the various aspects of this profession. Here is a summary of what can be said of a professional coach. A professional coach practices active listening, clear and direct communication, non-judgmental observation, asks powerful questions and has the capacity to hold a "safe space." These trained competencies are key pillars of the professional coaching process. The professional coach's mission is to accompany the coachee in discovering her or his own solutions, holding the belief that the coachee has the capacity to access the necessary resources. As we have demonstrated with the coachman/taxi driver, a coach guides and accompanies you *from your current situation to your desired one.* Whether you engage a coach on your own initiative or at the suggestion of your employer, the specific goals of your coaching engagement are mutually agreed between you and your coach at the outset.

Coach background: Professional coaches have also undergone sufficient self-awareness and self-development training to create an open and trustful space with coachees. With the support of a supervisor or mentor coach, certified coaches must regularly review and examine their coaching practices. Through the exploration and awareness of their own blind spots and filters of perception, coaches are more fully available to be with clients without judgment, and without conscious intent to influence. It is incumbent upon coaches to be aware of how and to what degree they interact and also what is and is not "allowed" in the frame of professional coaching.

In all cases where your needs as coachee or potential coachee are outside of the scope of the coach's responsibilities, the coach must clearly inform you and, where appropriate, propose other support, which may include therapy, medical monitoring or training. In short, your coach must be a professional!

Coaching is a profession in its own right that merits its independent place in business and in society at large. A major challenge of professional coach associations and federations is to ensure that clients can call on the services of true professional coaches. More than ever, the demands of such associations are to ensure verifiable standards for this burgeoning profession. Many other older professions - dentists, anesthesiologists, psychologists, teachers, etc. – have also experienced some vagueness in their initial stages, when in later stages the role becomes clear and indisputable. In today's turbulent and rapidly changing environment, professional coaching plays, and will continue to play, a vital role in the well-being of individuals and organizations.

As with any new and innovative profession, coaching has its own short-comings. Because regulation of the profession is not yet widespread, anyone can call themselves a coach, thus opening the door to great uncertainty for those who wish to engage a true professional. At the same time, coaching's spectacular evolution and its consequent positive impacts remain largely under-recognized. Except in the world of sports where athletes have benefited from the help of sports coaches for many years, professional coaching remains somewhat hidden, if not all together unknown in many areas. Fortunately, this trend is shifting! Recent statistics show there are more professional coaches who are worthy of this title. Correspondingly more and more organizations, companies and individuals are engaging professional coaches. (PwC, 2010)

Beyond a natural disposition and willingness to help others, the professional coach possesses both innate qualities and acquired skills, and at the same time respects professional ethics. In this book, we will consider **exclusively** the category of professional coaches who meet the specific criteria noted below.

TEN PLATINUM RULES OF THE PROFESSIONAL COACH

- is a humanist, client-centered, and profoundly interested in the well-being of all human beings
- believes each client is whole and unique
- has successfully completed coach-specific training through recognized coaching programs
- engages in ongoing personal development and professional training
- stays up to date on research and developments in the coaching profession and in human sciences
- has validated hours of qualified coaching with paying clients
- is a member in good standing of a professional group or association with defined professional competency standards and practices
- is bound by a professional code of ethics, a copy of which is available for potential and current clients
- regularly submits and reviews his or her coaching practice through supervision and/or mentor coaching
- holds a current certification/credential confirming all points above

WHAT CHANGE IS POSSIBLE WITH A COACH?

If you are interested in the world of sports, you have most likely heard champions speak of the coaches who helped them to achieve their best performance. Have you also noticed how often champions and winning teams thank their coaches when accepting their awards or medals or winning an important match?

Most often, the sports trainer works in collaboration with a sports coach to ensure not only physical preparedness but also their mental readiness. The coach focuses on a mindset that supports excellence. Similarly, people in search of job performance or greater satisfaction in life can be helped by a coach.

The coach with a small 'c' works to effect "level 1" changes

The coach with a small 'c' guides you to be more aware of your resources, your ability to change, to adapt, to challenge yourself in a particular situation and to adjust your behavior. This type of coaching is situational and is often referred to as a change of level 1 magnitude.

The coach with a capital 'C' works to effect change at "level 2"

The Coach with a capital 'C' helps you to effect more generative changes associated with different levels of your identity, such as strengthening self-awareness, self-esteem, self-confidence, and relational/social skills. Coaching at a deeper level helps to identify your core values, empowering or limiting beliefs, unique strengths, energy sources and key motivational factors. You are able to incorporate behavioral adjustments from a holistic approach and the work may touch on aspects of mind, body and spirit. The Coach who uses such an approach engages your full potential in a sustainable way which allows you to realize your dreams and aspirations as well as your professional goals. Such coaching corresponds to "level 2" change.

For more >>
Conversation with a coaching expert
www.professional-coaching.net

Where are professional coaches worldwide?
What are the characteristics of coaches?

- 47,500 professional coaches globally (compared to 30,000 in 2007)
- 15,800 in North America
- 17,800 in Western Europe
- 6.9 coaches per 1 million population

Characteristics:
Largest share (37%) of professional coaches is 46-55 years
- 9% less than 35 years
- 27% - 36 – 45 years
- 37% - 46 – 55 years
- 23% - 56 – 65 years
- 4% - over 65 years
The profile is younger in emerging regions

- 67% are women, 33% are men
- 60% have advanced or third level degrees, such as Masters or PhD
- 49% with more than 5 years' experience
- 19% with 10 or more years' experience (compared to 14% in 2006)

Results from recent PwC survey (PwC, 2012)

 Organizational coaching program in the words of the Director General of a global humanitarian organization

Coaching entered into our organizational strategy some years ago. Previously, we had experienced the limits of mentoring, that is to say, a more experienced employee in a field taking a novice under his/her wing. But the expected transfer of cultural awareness and relevant skills was not really up to our expectations; we wanted a deep alignment of our

teams to meet the requirements of our mission. We needed this and our management training did not consistently offer this skill development and transfer of knowledge that are essential to our success in rapidly evolving critical global environments.

Initially, we started to integrate 4 hours of one-to-one bilateral coaching for 700 senior leaders and managers. Given the success of this method in the following years, we strengthened the integration of coaching for managers assuming new roles and offer "transition" coaching from a pool of experienced certified professional coaches who are familiar with our culture.

At the time when we set up the pilot of our new leadership and people development program, the eyes turned to me and my busy schedule. I accepted my turn to work with a coach although I admit that initially it seemed absolutely unnecessary. It was one thing to recommend it to others and to see the benefits it brought them, and quite another to invest myself personally. As it turns out, this was a thought-provoking opportunity to clarify my vision and capacity to share. The coaching work undoubtedly contributed to my professional and personal development.

My Notes

SUMMARY
WHAT IS A PROFESSIONAL COACH?

✓ A coach is a professional practitioner of the helping profession. That is to say, the professional coach has validated coach-specific training and practice to accompany a client in professional development and personal growth.

✓ Coaching offers results and outcomes that equip clients to face challenges and opportunities today and in the future.

✓ Unlike the consultant, the coach does not provide the solution and does not advise the coachee what to do.

✓ Through the coaching process, the coach enables clients to find their own solution(s). In this manner, the professional coach is a catalyst of human potential and a learning facilitator.

✓ As in other professions, the professional coach adheres to a code of ethics and professional standards and applies them appropriately in all coaching situations.

Insanity is doing the same thing, over and over again, and expecting different results.
- Albert Einstein

2
WOULD HIRING A COACH BE USEFUL TO ME?

THE RHYTHM OF CHANGE IS ACCELERATING - IF NOT NOW, WHEN?

You have probably noticed things change with lightning speed and it is not easy or comfortable for most of us. Proof abounds all around us that the complexity of the world is accelerating faster than our evolution as a species. The 21st century invited us all into a frenzied and ever-changing dance. The challenge is often not only to adapt quickly but also to anticipate what's ahead. Life balance, which is so precious to our well-being, is increasingly difficult to find and maintain. In this age of digital communication, rapid and "unpredictable" change has become routine, sometimes for better and sometimes for worse.

Coaching responds to the need to innovate, to find new solutions and to know what to release. Are you among the many who:

- ☐ Need new skills to meet the challenges of an ever-changing workplace?
- ☐ Want to enhance personal growth and professional success?
- ☐ Want to feel more motivated and energized?
- ☐ Received feedback regarding the need to develop more Emotional Intelligence?
- ☐ Want to be more creative? More innovative? More solution-focused?
- ☐ Sometimes feel exhausted, ineffective or stuck?
- ☐ Want to be more productive and attain healthy life balance?
- ☐ Are experiencing personal or professional transitions?
- ☐ Reached a point where you want to clarify your life priorities?
- ☐ Feel the need to take a step back to gain new perspectives?
- ☐ **Are already doing well and are ready for a new challenge?**

You might have already experienced what it's like to change. Whether we choose it or external circumstances dictate, change is a source of discomfort, stress and resistance in varying degrees. Linked with other aspects of life - current situation, habits, personality and mindset - dealing with change is a tough test. Accompanying clients through such transformation is a common application for coaching and can be initiated on your own decision or your employer's.

Professional coaching is relevant for physically and psychologically healthy people who have a desire to go beyond, to progress and to develop themselves personally or professionally. For a pre-determined length of time, your coach supports you to reach your specific and agreed objectives.

ICF defines coaching as...

partnering with clients in a thought-provoking and creative process that inspires them to maximize their personal and professional potential even in the face of growing complexity and uncertainty.

WHERE AND WHEN CAN A COACH BE USEFUL?

Coaching can be helpful in a wide variety of contexts. See if one or more of these situations resonates with you:

- ☐ Preparing for a new job, new responsibilities, new environment
- ☐ Organization is downsizing and you need to improve workplace skills: communication, conflict resolution, public speaking, working across a matrix organization
- ☐ Just received team feedback and you need to develop greater self-awareness and resilience
- ☐ Facing changing economic conditions and need to rethink your career
- ☐ Feeling the need to clarify personal and professional goals
- ☐ Experiencing cross-cultural issues and need to get results in a matrix organization

- ☐ Sensing overload and the need to better manage stress and develop emotional intelligence
- ☐ Spending too much time working and need better life balance
- ☐ Want to start a new business
- ☐ Leading a dynamic team and need to enhance self-confidence and executive presence
- ☐ Facing the need to develop strategic vision and solution-oriented thinking
- ☐ Teams merging and need to improve performance and team effectiveness
- ☐ Nearing retirement and need to implement a succession plan

What is the profile of coaching clients?

- 54% are women, 46% are men
- 65% are under 46 (55% in North America, 87% in Eastern Europe)
  The age profile tends to be younger in the emerging regions
- 69% are managers, executives or entrepreneurs
- 21% are private clients

Main areas addressed in coaching engagements

- 38% personal development
- 32% interpersonal relationships
- 28% self-esteem – self confidence
- 26% communication skills
- 26% staff/team effectiveness
- 25% work-life balance

Results from recent PwC survey (PwC, 2012)

WHICH COACH FITS YOUR CURRENT SITUATION?

When meeting a coach, you may be curious to ask, "What kind of coach are you?" And indeed this is a valid and relevant question as you will soon discover a wide range of coaching specialties. More than this, you will also realize that coaches are often creative, curious and open to new approaches and techniques. These new discoveries may appear on the coach's list of services offered. To keep it simple, bear in mind that you can distinguish three basic categories of coaching: life, career, corporate.

I. Three main categories of coaching

Coaching Categories	Types of Coaching	Themes –some examples
Life Coaching	Life coaching Health and wellness Life transitions	Family, couple Life balance Stress management Spirituality Retirement
Career Coaching	Professional development Career planning	New job Work-life balance Self-confidence New behaviors Career transition
Corporate Coaching, Executive Coaching, Business Coaching	Organizational coaching Executive coaching Team coaching	Organizational Leadership Relationships Communication Team effectiveness

Different types of coaching respond to different situations

◌ *I have a dilemma and need to consider more options!*

Life coaching. You want to engage in a personal development process. Your objective concerns family, partners, friends or other personal relationships, spirituality, life purpose, fulfillment or a wide variety of other personal situations. At this point, we need to mention that each type of coaching at one point or another could address these subjects. The heart of the coaching process increases self-awareness, improves interpersonal relationships, and broadens understanding of the world we live in.

I will retire soon - I want to get ready!

Life transition coaching. You go through a major transition: a new relationship, divorce, birth of a child, grief, entering, re-entering or leaving the workplace. All these changes can be effectively facilitated through appropriate and specialized coaching.

I want to be healthier - I need help!

Wellness, health, sports coaching. In these situations, you might also engage a doctor, nutritionist, naturopath, or sports trainer, in parallel to professional coaching in order to achieve your goal. For example, if you want to stop smoking, lose weight, reduce stress, you may benefit from working with a medical expert as well as a professional coach.

I have an idea but I keep getting stuck!

Somatic Coaching. The word somatic comes from the Greek root soma, which means "the living body in its wholeness." Somatic coaching invites a way to observe and create holistic awareness. It is a process in which one embodies new practices, that is to say, paying attention to movements, postures, and sensations. This approach is highly effective when you are stuck or unable to pinpoint what is not working. Somatic coaching techniques employ physical movement to unblock autonomous or automatic pilot patterns of thinking, feeling, and behaving. It is not so much about feeling better, it is more about getting better at feeling and sensing.

⌇ *I am looking for a new job - I need to get focused!*

Career Coaching. This includes behavioral skills at work: communication skills, presentation skills, professional or "executive" presence, priority management, stress reduction and the full range of management competencies. This form of coaching is particularly useful in career transitions, whether the change is by choice or necessity. Career coaching helps to develop self-awareness, self-confidence, prepare for job interviews, identify new directions, recognize opportunities, or get ready to return to work after an extended pause. Assessments and other tools are sometimes used to measure the effectiveness and capabilities before and after working with a career coach.

⌇ *I want to boost my business skills - I need an action plan!*

Business coaching. The majority of business coaches themselves have previous business experience and consequently an understanding of the demands of the business world. The business coach accompanies the manager and sometimes the manager's team to achieve their individual, team and organizational objectives, while simultaneously developing the competences and skills of the individuals. With the express agreement of the coachee, this form of coaching tends to be more directive and can include suggestions or examples. As with other categories of coaching, the relationship between coachee and coach is paramount. The business coach partners with the manager to achieve business specific outcomes, identify strategies, explore opportunities and risks, and define action plans. The coach may act as "shadow coach" to observe the manager in action throughout the workday and offer feedback around interactions between and among team members, as well as with external partners.

⌇ *I want to be an inspiring leader with a vision and followers!*

Executive Coaching. Executive coaching is one of the fastest growing segments of professional coaching. Working with executives and top leaders, this type of coaching focuses on developing leadership competencies around communication, innovation, creativity, strategic thinking, visioning, decision making, achieving organizational goals, external relations, directing the work of others and developing talent.

The executive coach is often expected to have relevant prior experience in order to better grasp the organizational context and highly complex, global environments of their executive clients. Coaching leaders at this level is often a mix of personal and leadership development, relational skills and business achievement and requires a global approach given the importance and scope of the executive's responsibilities. Confidentiality and discretion are of utmost importance as with other forms of coaching.

As mentioned above in business coaching, executive coaching often includes more directive elements, particularly around the theme of informed questioning and direct feedback/feed-forward. Again "shadow coaching" is an effective process to enable the client to benefit from the external perspective and experience of the coach. The coach serves as a confidential "sounding board" and often engages in role plays to help the client practice and prepare for important meetings, conversations or presentations. Much like top athletes, the executive must perform consistently and at the highest levels, and an executive coach can play a vital role in this often intense and fast-paced environment.

Other specialties

You have no doubt understood by now that you are likely to meet coaches who work in areas outside of those listed above; for example, teens, expats, lawyers, artists, teachers, politicians, spirituality, etc. The specialty list is long. In each case, the coach has specific experience and training with related accreditations and qualifications. You may find coaches who are trained in mindfulness, body movement or relaxation practices to reduce stress, increase concentration and enhance wellbeing.

As a human being, you are naturally unique and complex, and so is each coach. Before hiring a coach you must be clear where you want to work with a coach. You can easily imagine that throughout your life you may find the need to engage a coach with specialties in any number of the areas mentioned above. The successful outcome of coaching relies enormously on the match between the need of the coachee and the specificity of the coach. Long-term coaching success depends on both immediate chemistry and trustful relationship between coach and coachee.

We hope this chapter provides you a better understanding of the world of professional coaching.

Main coaching specialties

- 58% business coaching (leadership, business/organizational, executive)
- 13% life vision and enhancement
- 7% career
- 2% relationships
- 2% health and fitness
- 6% miscellaneous
- 7% others
- 3% no specialty

Results from recent PwC survey (PwC, 2012)

ARE YOU READY FOR COACHING NOW?

We invite you now to check if you are ready for coaching or for something else. Please answer: YES or NO or I DON'T KNOW.

I feel well physically and psychologically

Yes ❑   No ❑   I don't know ❑

I want to prioritize what is most important to me but I have no time!

Yes ❑   No ❑   I don't know ❑

I am prepared to invest what it takes to ensure coaching is successful.

Yes ❑   No ❑   I don't know ❑

I am interested to know myself better.

Yes ❑   No ❑   I don't know ❑

I want more time for myself.

Yes ❑   No ❑   I don't know ❑

I am curious to explore new options and opportunities.

Yes ❑   No ❑   I don't know ❑

I would like to better understand my values and strengths.

Yes ❑   No ❑   I don't know ❑

I would like some support to move through a challenging situation.

Yes ❑   No ❑   I don't know ❑

I am a bit confused and would like more clarity.

Yes ❑   No ❑   I don't know ❑

I see the value to engage a professional as a "sounding board."

Yes ❑   No ❑   I don't know ❑

I think there are solutions for my problems or current situation.

Yes ❑   No ❑   I don't know ❑

I would like to get to the next level at work/in my career.

Yes ❑   No ❑   I don't know ❑

I believe that I can improve my relationships with others.

Yes ❑   No ❑   I don't know ❑

I want to feel more harmony and balance in my life.

Yes ❑   No ❑   I don't know ❑

Results

- If you answered "Yes" to most of these statements, you can consider yourself ready for coaching.
- If you answered "I don't know" or "No" to the majority of these statements, we suggest you give yourself time for additional reflection before you decide to engage a coach or explore other options.

In short, this exercise is designed to help you decide if your current situation is best served by hiring a coach or engaging another source of support that may be more appropriate.

A confusing starting point

For ten years, Tom was a member of a sales team of twenty in a multinational agribusiness. Up to now, he had always performed well, enjoyed excellent relations with George, his ex-team leader, and with the other team members. He had seniority and assumed that he was George's natural successor when he retired. Regardless of his strong lobbying to get the position, upper management and human resources did not have the same opinion and he was not promoted.

Not only was he extremely disappointed but also the relationship with his new manager was very difficult. Simultaneously he wanted to quit but was afraid to be out of work. He was afraid of being fired, even though he felt it was deeply unfair given his many years of loyal service.

HR engaged a professional coach to work with Tom, but he was not at all clear what a coach could do for him at this point. His feelings of anger and betrayal prevented him from understanding how to go forward. The coach's role was to help him clarify the current situation and determine a reasonable and positive way forward. Through the coaching process, Tom became aware of various situations that were blocking him. He had a false perception of the situation and had to let go of and mourn this missed promotion. He needed to take another look at his professional capabilities, identify his strengths and restore his self-confidence, while re-establishing a healthy relationship with his new manager.

With the resources he developed through coaching, he was able to make satisfying decisions and identify medium and long-term solutions.

For more >>
"How Coaching Works"
video with the permission of Well Coaches
www.professional-coaching.net

SUMMARY
WOULD HIRING A COACH BE USEFUL TO ME?

✓ **Time**: In rapidly changes times, new actions require new thinking and new ways of being.

✓ **Situations and fit with coach**: Coaching is useful in a variety of situations, such as achieving personal and professional objectives and goals, identifying and maximizing your resources, and realizing your full potential.

✓ **Your particular situation** will be best served by a specific type of coaching. And the three broad categories of coaching are life, career and corporate/business/executive.

If you don't like something, change it.
If you can't change it, change your attitude.
- Maya Angelou

3
IF NOT A COACH, WHO COULD HELP ME?

DID YOU CONSIDER A CONSULTANT, MENTOR, THERAPIST, OR TRAINING?

No doubt for us, the coaching process is a highly useful and powerful approach, but it is not the only one. It seems fair to describe here other types of support to help you make the best possible choice. Depending on your specific needs, another supporting relationship may be more appropriate.

The starting point is to understand the nature of your objective. During a first interview, your coach should be ready to discuss the various approaches and evaluate if the need exists to direct you to another professional or to suggest a parallel approach with coaching.

Most coaches maintain relationships with other helping professionals, including therapists and psychologists. We do this for two reasons. First, for our own professional development to learn and share ideas with individuals with specific expertise; and second, these relationships serve as a referral network to better serve our clients.

In some client-coach relationships, an issue comes up that sits outside the coach's area of expertise or qualifications. In such situations, the coach tells you that the issue is not something the coach is capable or qualified to address, and asks how you would like to address the issue. If you are open to considering more appropriate assistance, the coach can often make a referral.

Here is a quick overview of some other professions that can be complementary to the coaching process.

What can a consultant or other expert do for me?

Consultants or experts can be useful in their specific field of expertise, where they have confirmed knowledge and skills. They could help you by giving advice, proposing solutions or defining choices. In technical fields, this is often a highly useful source of assistance. However, on a personal level, even 'good' advice is rarely effective. For example, if you want to organize your inheritance, a notary or lawyer can help you. These professionals can tell you how to do things properly where a coach is not qualified to do so. On the other hand, a coach will help you clarify what is really important to you (and your family) and will accompany you through the process to arrive at a clear decision on what distribution suits you best.

Will a mentor be a role model for me?

A mentor offers guidance, advice and examples from her or his own experience or career. In particular, a mentor is someone who has already become successful in the area where you seek assistance. In fact, you may have already had a mentor without using this term. You could have been positively influenced by someone's example and experiences. You may have learned from your mentor's achievements and successes, and you listened to the examples and advice with conviction, while at the same time knowing a mentor is not a guru. Your mentor could be a teacher, a manager or work colleague, a family member or a friend. Mentors act as role models for one or more behaviors. Today, we find mentors using a "coach approach," meaning that they provide less advice, and offer more challenge to help you define your own conclusions and solutions.

What if I need a therapist, psychotherapist, psychologist, psychiatrist or other medical professional?

This is a fundamental question that your coach must explore during the first meeting. In general, coaching is future oriented, while therapy often addresses healing pain and dysfunctions rooting in the past. If you are suffering deeply, various forms of therapy may be a more appropriate approach. There are enough examples of approaches to fill an encyclopedia with details and nuances. Mental disorders, their associated treatments and psychiatric disorders are best served by members of the medical profession rather than coaching. Psychiatrists are medical doctors, who can diagnose disorders and disease and are also able to prescribe medication as part of the overall treatment program. Here we touch on an extremely important point. The **professional coach code of ethics** refers to the coach's competency to recognize the need and to provide the appropriate direction to a client if necessary.

⌒ *Who will teach me new skills and knowledge? A trainer?*

The trainer is perhaps the most familiar to you. Training is based on certain learning objectives delivered according to a pre-determined curriculum. Coaching is customized to each client rather than following a fixed curriculum. Indeed, trainers can teach knowledge and competencies in their area(s) of expertise. Particularly in business, a trainer is hired to teach technical skills, such as computer science, IT technology, languages, and also soft skills, such as communication, management, and leadership. In some cases, coaching complements training. As many statistics and firsthand experience prove, knowing *about* something is not the same as knowing *how* to do something. Coaching that follows training has been proven many times to improve knowledge retention and on-the-job application of the training and increases the return on investment (ROI) on the investment in training.

IS IT ONLY A PROFESSIONAL WHO CAN HELP?

Apart from professionals who are hired under a business contract, you've probably experienced more spontaneous ways to get help. By nature, we human beings are driven to help and support each other. For sure, trained professionals are not the only source of help. Quite naturally, you get support from family, friends, community, etc. This is another source of invaluable and essential help.

⌒ *How can I use peer coaching or co-coaching?*

In this approach, you are not necessarily limited to interacting with someone in your immediate environment. Online or in person, you can find help by joining a network of individuals facing the same issue or challenge, or who have similar interests.

One-to-one or in social network groups, it is possible to apply the principles of coaching. By choosing a common focus, various coaching methodologies can be applied. Co-coaching or peer coaching can help stimulate motivation and establish momentum to achieve a common goal, such as job search.

With a peer you give and receive mutual support. Peer coaching can be particularly useful in a business setting. A well-chosen peer can offer an objective view, act as a thinking partner and encourage your accountability. It is also worth noting that some clear risks exist in peer coaching, such as falling into commiserating: "We'll never get management to change, that's just the way things are here!", or giving advice that can be self-serving or even detrimental: "In your place, I'd do this and not that."

You need to exercise discernment, distinguish between coaching and advice giving and. at all times, take care to retain your capacity for independent analysis and decision making.

ꛥ *With self-coaching, I coach myself. Does it work?*
This approach is just what it implies: to coach oneself by:

- giving yourself time to step back and reflect in a structured way
- using self-questioning techniques
- setting aside regular time in your agenda for this process

Self-coaching resources can be found online and in a wide variety of books and other publications. By calling on your "inner coach," you can keep a journal, evaluate your progress, observe your thoughts, feelings and sensations, be aware of your emotions and learn to name and manage them.

If, in principle, we are all equipped for self-coaching and, if this approach is efficient both in terms of time and money, self-compassion is rare and not always available. And self-compassion and self-awareness are essential for successful self-coaching! Any time that you invite your inner coach, you also need to quiet your inner critic and quell self-critical thought patterns. Being aware and non-judgmental and keeping the promises that we make to ourselves are not easy. Like exercising at the gym, going it alone requires discipline, commitment and strong motivation over an extended period, while joining a class or hiring a personal trainer provides added support and stimulation. In essence, with self-coaching, you are required to act as both coach and coachee.

As you see, self-coaching has its limitations. Self-coaching, as well as peer coaching, are excellent regular practices that do not preclude working with a professional coach.

WHAT OTHER EXPERTISE COULD PROFESSIONAL COACHES HAVE?

The coach's previous professional experience, especially in business, brings expertise that can be provided in parallel to coaching. Depending on the client's requests, some coaches also offer consulting, training, facilitation or mentoring under separate and discreet mandates. This wider set of skills and approaches defines and differentiates coaches and their specialties.

Coaching "purists" advocate that coaches do not give advice, train or consult as part of the coaching process. In reality, some coaches offer mixed support and it is advisable to clarify your expectations with the coach up front.

For example, following team management training, coaching conversations may reinforce the learning around mastering applications on the job, self-confidence and self-esteem. In another situation, and with your express permission, a coach could assume a more directive role at some point in a coaching session. This might include sharing previous experience, giving you examples to help you be more creative, more critical, but will return to the coaching process through questioning how you can use this information in your specific situation. With your express permission to speak outside the coaching role, your coach might also offer you another perspective in their realm of expertise.

Coaching is designed to raise your awareness and to help you identify new perspectives and find new solutions. You will find coaches who take a more non-directive approach: asking questions and offering observations to create new awareness and leaving the space for you to take your decisions. You will also find coaches who use a more directive approach and may suggest possible solutions or offer advice. Finding the appropriate balance is a critical element of "fit" with your coach - both at the outset and at any point during the coaching process.

Coaching must remain the dominant mode of any coaching intervention. As we have seen in many cases, coaches employ a range of approaches and may wear a number of "hats" depending on the circumstances and the coach's expertise. But in all cases where there is a coaching contract, professional coaching must remain the predominant mode of delivery.

Any additional services combined with coaching should be discussed with you in advance, clearly defined and your permission agreed, before your coach "changes hats."

This is a critical ethical point that you and your coach should bear in mind. If the coach has not asked for and received permission to use approaches other than coaching, this can undermine the coaching process. Similarly, if you do not understand the different roles that the coach can assume, you will not know what to ask and how to grant, or not, permission to the coach to use other techniques. As we have already mentioned, in actual practice, coaching is a sophisticated blend of techniques and approaches – all with the aim to position you, the coachee, as the decision maker and expert of your situation. This mixture of approaches may be mentioned in a written contract or by verbal agreement. In general coaching provides non-directive support where the core coaching competencies are applied. (see p.66)

Almost all coaches (94%) offer one or more services <u>in addition to coaching</u> within their overall professional practice

- 62% consulting
- 60% training
- 50% facilitation
- 29% teaching
- 4% mentoring

Results from recent PwC survey (PwC, 2012)

Client facing a mixed and varied situation

When Nadia married Mike, an Executive Director in the banking sector, she was responsible for event planning in a communication company based in Munich. Mike received a promotion and Nadia simultaneously decided to quit her job and move to Geneva with her husband. They have two children and are expecting a third. Nadia decides to dedicate herself to her family and to take time to settle into this new country for the benefit of the family.

Three years later, when the youngest starts pre-school, Nadia sets out to find a job. Mike is often away and the responsibility for their home falls mainly on her. She is a woman of action and commitment, and is tireless in her job search. She had no idea she would encounter so many difficulties. The event planning market seems saturated and few jobs match her profile. She even removed several degrees on her CV so she would not hear again that she is "overqualified." Although she spares no effort, after multiple unsuccessful interviews her morale eventually begins to suffer. Gradually, she views the various stages of recruitment as tests and then as personal failures. Nonetheless she continues to battle each day, meeting new people, and spending hours on the internet.

She is becoming increasingly stressed, cannot sleep and is often tearful. She decides to hire a coach to help her find a job. From the first meeting, when describing the efforts she has undergone, she collapses in tears. Her coach makes her aware of her state of exhaustion and of the priority to seek treatment. She agrees and goes to a doctor who diagnoses a burn-out and prescribes treatment and monitoring. But her determination to find a job is always present; her coach then accompanies her in this research, while ensuring she continues her medical treatment for burn-out.

Physical and psychological health is essential for effective coaching. Once she sufficiently recovered her health, Nadia was able to engage in the coaching process, working both on an action plan to return to work and supported by in-depth work on her confidence and self-image. A few months later, she found a job that was not quite in line with her expectations, and a year later found another where she continues to flourish.

SUMMARY
IF NOT A COACH, WHO COULD HELP ME?

✓ Depending on your needs, you can engage a consultant, mentor, therapist, trainer or other professional. You can work independently (self-coaching), with a colleague or a group of people with similar needs (peer coaching).

✓ Even if a professional coach offers complementary expertise (consulting, training, mentoring), coaching remains the predominant approach.

✓ The primary focus of coaching is to generate actionable strategies and to achieve specific objectives.

The greatest part of our happiness or misery depends on our dispositions and not on our circumstances.
- Martha Washington

4
HOW CAN I FIND MY COACH?

You will certainly find a coach who is well-suited for you by taking a few recommended steps before making your choice. Each client is unique, every coach is unique and it is important to find *your* coach, the one who can help you achieve your objectives and fits with the style, pace and approach that suits you.

For your coach, as for your hair dresser or dentist, you would assume that training, skills, experience, and reputation help to guarantee professionalism. Almost anyone can call themselves a "coach," so it is up to you to sharpen your knowledge of the skills and other requirements for this mandate. To begin, a selection phase is necessary.

Above all, the relationship between you and your coach is the key success ingredient of your coaching experience.

◌ *How and where do I find the coach to match my needs?*

It is worth investing time in this selection step especially considering the increasing number of coaches and those pretending to be coaches.

In general, the internet and social networks are an inexhaustible source of information. Many coaches' websites describe their profile, expertise, experience, training, specialties, and a multitude of other details. The coach's website is literally a window into their world – and a good place to start your research.

Word of mouth is also useful selection criteria. Although not everyone volunteers who or why they engaged a professional coach, you might find some friends or colleagues who have previously hired a coach. When this information is offered, it is current and often provides relevant input.

Many human resources departments are already working with coaches and could propose a coach that suits you. Often coaches in your organization's "coaching pool" have been pre-screened and have some experience in your environment.

Even where you do not have specific recommendations, you have a great opportunity to find your coach among the members of professional coach associations or qualified coaching schools. These institutions have lists of coach references based on their established criteria.

Even before a first meeting, you can find some valuable information about the coach's style, approach to coaching, values, typical clients, partners, achievements, etc. You will already have identified some important information, such as: your coach's specific training, prior experience, expertise, degree, accreditation, and professional affiliations. Because every coaching relationship is a unique partnership, you are best served to prepare a list of relevant questions in advance of your first meeting.

GETTING TO KNOW THE COACH YOU MEET

If this is the first time you are hiring a coach and your coach has not been specifically recommended to you, you might consider speaking with two coaches before making your final choice. Do not be hesitant or shy. A professional is also interested to ensure a fit for both of you. This exploratory dialogue is usually free and is often not considered a coaching session. It is a good idea to clarify this point before speaking with any potential coach.

This first meeting is crucial. Do take the time to check the chemistry with any potential coach.

II. Important information to inquire about your coach

Areas	Criteria
Training	School, program, duration
Accreditation or credential	Local or international recognition
Professional experience	Seniority, achievements, awards
Professional association membership	Federation, association, schools
Ethical & professional standards	Code of Ethics
Confidentiality	Corporate or institutional confidentiality clauses
Style	Approaches, methods, models
Supervision / mentor coaching	The supervisor of the coach
Continuing education and training	Themes, primary interests of study and research
Coaching rates and programs	Program, rates, contract, agreement

Some useful questions to ask during an initial conversation.

☌ *What coach-specific training have you followed?*

The duration of the coach-specific training is important – there is a huge difference between a course of a few hours and a program over several years. Given the many coaching schools and programs, including online and distance-learning, it may be useful to check the credibility of your potential coach's training. For most valid training, the participant who successfully meets the course criteria obtains a certificate or diploma. Often these diplomas or certificates are displayed in the coach's office. Recently, coaching is also taught in universities and business schools. ICF approves training globally and all ICF-approved coach training programs are specifically dedicated to the 11 core competencies of professional coaching and to the personal development of the coach (see p.66). These two aspects assure consistent and high quality coach training.

☌ *What certification do you have? What does it represent?*

Accreditation is one of the key ways for coaches to demonstrate a guarantee of professionalism. The current and pervasive trend is to strengthen the standards of the profession in order to ensure clients a reliable coaching, whether for individuals on their own or in organizations. Suddenly, "accreditations" are everywhere. Here is how you navigate this crowded environment.

Most coaching programs award a certificate or diploma that attests to the training. These documents are issued following successful completion of written and oral exams, a memoire or case study. In some locations, local federations or associations also offer a coaching accreditation process. But beyond the attractive certificate on the wall, it is worthwhile to ask your coach about the criteria of such accreditation.

At the global level, several organizations award credentials. Among these, ICF has issued one of the three levels of credentials to more than 10,000 coaches worldwide and continues to receive applications regularly. Each ICF credential is based on the number and quality of coach-specific training hours, training and demonstrated proficiency of the eleven core competencies and the requisite number of hours with paying clients. The ICF accreditations are awarded for three years and require renewal by completing continuing education hours as well as hours of supervision or mentor coaching.

III. ICF Credential criteria
(example of portfolio certification)

Credential Requirements	Training Hours	Coaching Experience Hours	Supervision Hours	Min. Number Clients	Exam to validate coaching level of 11 Core Competencies
ACC Associate Certified Coach	60	100	10	8	Must meet ACC minimum requirements
PCC Professional Certified Coach	125	750	10	25	Must meet minimum PCC requirements
MCC Master Certified Coach	200	2 500	10	35	Must meet minimum MCC requirements

As in any other profession, the certification or credential alone, whatever it is, does not guarantee talent or fit. The ICF accreditation takes into account the experience of the coach with paying clients and is a reliable criterion of expertise. These three levels of certification/accreditation are increasingly seen by organizations as a guarantee of professionalism to recruit coaches.

As the leading professional coach association, ICF reviews and evolves the credentialing process. From time to time the specific criteria are modified in line with changing requirements of the profession.

Training and practice over time, keeping up to date on relevant research and applications for coaching and ongoing self-development are important measures for maintaining high professional standards.

✑ *What is your prior experience and background?*

Your coach's previous professional activity, life experience, philosophy and interests may have an impact on your coaching relationship. The relationship with your coach is based on mutual trust and confidentiality. It is therefore natural that you know something about your coach's background.

The coach's typical clients are also strong indicators. It is important to note there is great diversity in areas where coaching is used successfully: executive coaching, business, leadership, life, career, etc. You can also inquire about the strengths, focus areas and some typical coaching situations to find a fit with your expectations and needs.

✑ *What professional networks or associations do you belong to and why?*

Considering the lack of formal legislation in most markets, membership in a professional association is a reliable gauge to help discern the seriousness and rigor of your coach. Each network, federation or association of coaches, establishes standards of the coaching profession to which your coach adheres. You can visit the websites of the various associations to see for yourself the specific criteria. As for coach training networks, association networks can be composed of local, national, regional or global coaches.

✑ *Are you bound by a professional code of ethics?*

In any helping professional, ethical behavior should be clearly described and respected. How to behave as a coach should not depend on the sole discretion of the individual coach. Choosing a coach who abides by a recognized code of ethics is a good way to avoid charlatans, gurus and fake shrinks. By joining a professional association or federation, your coach has signed and committed to a strict code of ethics. This guarantees a high standard of ethical practices. It also allows you to register a complaint to the professional association in case of major problems or abuse (e.g., ICF Independent Review Board).

◯ *How do you manage confidentiality?*

As with social networks, details of your private life can move around the globe in seconds. It is essential that strict confidentiality is honored by your coach. In the case where your organization is funding your coaching, the situation needs clarifying before the coaching starts.

In this type of arrangement, each party - organization or company sponsor, coach, and coachee - agrees in advance what information is transmitted and what is not. In this regard, all codes of ethics include specific guidance on confidentiality. You can ask specifically about such things as record keeping, submission of a report and computer security, if you feel the need.

◯ *How would you describe your coaching style?*

A multitude of coaching styles, practices and approaches exists. Couple this with an even greater variety of personalities among coaches, and you have the opportunity to find a unique fit for your situation. **Finding a good fit is essential for effective coaching**. Ask your coach to describe the basic structure of the coaching process to make sure her or his style encourages you to commit yourself with confidence to working with this coach.

◯ *When did you last hire a supervisor or mentor coach?*

Simply put, you can imagine the supervisor or mentor coach as the coach's coach for their coaching practices, rather than any personal or professional issues the coach might address with another professional coach. As talented as your coach may be, he or she is not immune to acquiring blind spots or incorporating less productive habits over time. As many well-being professional practitioners, the certified coach must regularly challenge and seek support for continued professional development. Professional ethics require that the coach engages a supervisor or mentor coach to help validate the coach's practice and way of being with clients. In short this supervision is intended to ensure a more effective coach.

How do we evaluate my progress?

Coaches use various measures before and after the coaching process to assess your progress. These can include formal assessment tools, such as self-assessments, 360° questionnaires, key stakeholder interviews, or less formal tools as a reflection journal or satisfaction scales. The results of these exercises can help you evaluate your personal and professional learning and development.

What timing and structure do you suggest?

After your first coaching session and depending on your specific objectives, the coach has the expertise to recommend timing and frequency. The two of you then agree on the number and frequency of sessions, and what, if any, adjustments can be made during the coaching. Between each session, you will often be asked to commit to "homework," practice or reflection. Sessions can take place in person, by phone or internet (VOIP – voice over internet) or video conference. You may also exchange via email or instant messaging. Often a combination of these methods is used to complement your learning between sessions.

Do you have any special packages or inclusive offers?

According to your objectives and the specialty of the coach, the coach may offer additional options to support the process. These can be assessments or measurement tools mentioned above or other learning or support materials. Taking into consideration your needs, your coach may offer a lump sum or program fee that includes not only coaching sessions when you are together, but also work before and after each session. This program fee therefore corresponds to a total package and cannot be reduced to an hourly rate. For example, senior executives are frequently offered a coaching package designed to optimize the first 100 days in a new position.

What are your rates? What kind of contract do you offer?

Your coaching agreement is like any other business contract and follows the same rules. Your coach must clearly inform you of fees, terms and indicating any additional services agreed between the two of you. In all cases, you should receive a contract clearly stating the points of agreement: overall cost, process, location, duration, objectives, payment terms, coaching modalities, cancellation policies, and mutual agreement if your organization is an agent or sponsor. Transparency, honesty and authenticity must be standard operating procedure for professional coaching. With these elements in place, simple common sense will allow you to monitor the progress of the contract or agreement.

BETWEEN TWO COACHES, HOW DO YOU CHOOSE?

At this stage, you have made your pre-selection and you have met one or two coaches and have inquired about their professional standards. It is time to call on your intuition and personal impressions.

In choosing a coach, as with any other choice of service provider, your first impression counts and can be very reliable. But sometimes our subconscious plays tricks on us and we choose the coach who represents the path of least resistance. The following questions help you become aware of your impressions and decision making process. This exercise is an excellent precursor to coaching.

⌕ *How can I tap into my first impressions and intuition?*

- ☐ How did I feel during the first meeting?
- ☐ What level of confidence did I experience during this meeting?
- ☐ What do I appreciate about the coach's manner of communicating and personal style?
- ☐ Did I have the impression of speaking with a credible partner?
- ☐ Did the coach help to clarify my needs, my objectives?
- ☐ Did I feel challenged, supported, encouraged, inspired?
- ☐ Do I feel the coach is a good fit for the coaching journey?

What is most important to clients

- 93% Effectiveness of coaching process
- 92% Personal rapport between client and coach
- 80% Personal referrals
- 78% Explanation of coaching process
- 78% Client references and reputation of coach
- 66% Level of coach-specific training
- 62% Cost of coaching
- 55% Coaching experience in industry
- 53% Curriculum vitae (CV) or resume
- 52% Level of formal education/training

74% of individuals and organizations who use coaching expect their coaches to be certified or credentialed!

Results from recent PwC survey (PwC, 2012)

 The testimony of John, director and founder of a moving company

I was barely 25 years old when I had the opportunity to buy a truck. Then I hired a friend to collaborate with me to start a moving company. Those were the good times. In less than ten years, I had twenty trucks and more than sixty employees. Then I franchised my brand and we became nationally known and expanded internationally. I was proud of this success and at the same time I recognize now that I was afraid and almost could not believe it. In an almost offhand way, a friend of a friend of my wife said at a dinner party, "I see, John, you are breaking barriers and entering into a whole new world. I hope you have a good coach"

I'm the type to strike while the iron is hot. The next day I made an appointment with a coach who was available and located in the same city. I was almost fifty years old and I think he was too. He was full of energy and at the same time I had the feeling he was from another era. I felt a bit confused by his new age approach at the same time I was curious. We met in my office five or six times and each time I was even more confused. He talked about things that I didn't understand and that made me a bit uncomfortable. It seemed he was asking questions randomly - a bit of everything and nothing. He asked me to talk about "problems" that I didn't think were problems! After the last session, I found it hard to explain what we did together and still am not sure how it was helpful. Because of this experience, I must admit that I had a bad opinion of coaching. I had the impression coaching was about smoke and mirrors and that people like me could not grasp it. I mean people who have to make decisions and organize things concretely.

Time has passed, my business continued to thrive and I met another coach at a business meeting with whom I recounted my coaching experience with a touch of irony and cynicism. Just as I was about to take a drink, I was stopped by questions from this coach: "What did you need and that you didn't have?" And a little later in the discussion, she asked:" What do you want to achieve now?" It took me time to digest these questions and in fact they continued to turn in my head. Clearly I wanted to see this coach again. Following her suggestion to structure our sessions, we set an objective and I signed the coaching agreement. Over the next year, we met at a more or less regular rhythm in which I engaged in deep reflection around my personal values and my company objectives. In particular I was interested to better understand the drivers of my business and how I could continue to develop my business sustainably.

This set of objectives and the time to reflect with my coach were really indispensable to me personally and helped guide my business decisions for the future. I am sincerely grateful to my coach for this journey that allowed me to grow and strengthen the feeling of having access to my "best self". It has been a unique opportunity to fulfill myself personally and professionally. I can even say that my newfound empathy enriched the well-being of my employees and my family. I finally feel more peace of mind and I am more closely aligned with what is truly important to me. No more, no less!'

SUMMARY
HOW CAN I FIND MY COACH?

✓ Make an initial selection criteria list.
✓ Check with friends and colleagues, your human resources department, and professional associations, such as ICF.
✓ Have a conversation with the potential coach(s).
✓ Be sure to ask questions about the coach's practice, training, certifications, approaches, etc.
✓ Consider your first impressions.
✓ Make your choice and ask for written agreement from the chosen coach.
✓ Get started!

It is not because things are difficult that we do not dare,
it is because we do not dare that things are difficult.
- Seneca

5
HOW DOES COACHING WORK?

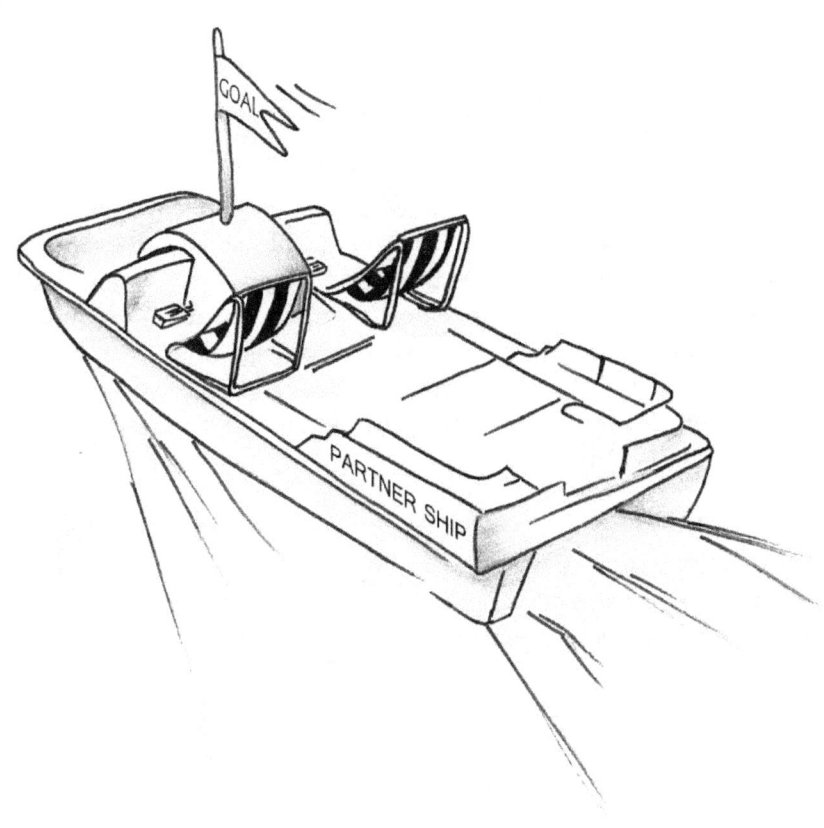

LET'S VISIT THE OVERALL COACHING PROCESS

Chemistry Meeting

Coaching is a structured, constructive conversation between coach and coachee incorporating a client-focused approach. The chemistry between the two is paramount. This meeting allows you to experience the type of conversation, the flow, pace and content of the coach's interaction with you and whether this suits you or not.

The Written Agreement

The details agreed verbally must be converted to a written contract or agreement to be signed jointly by you and your coach. (see example Coaching Agreement on p.52.) For coaching sponsored by your organization, your supervisor or human resources representative may also validate and sign the "tripartite" agreement.

Your First Session

Now you are on the starting line of coaching. You have chosen your coach and coaching can begin. This contact allows you to explore your needs, clarify your main objectives and begin the overall coaching process. Such elements as logistics, location, duration, frequency of meetings are discussed and confirmed. If this coaching was recommended by your organization, your supervisor or human resources representative may also be present for a portion of this session to clarify expectations.

The Process

Your coaching work starts here in line with the agreement. Coaching sessions take place one-to-one, in person, by phone, internet or email. Session by session your coach will accompany you to:

- Clarify your goals and objectives
- Identify your resources and strengths
- Acquire knowledge and new perspectives
- Practice new behaviors and discover opportunities
- Overcome obstacles and hindrances
- Agree and integrate an action plan

Your coach invites you to explore various new ways of thinking and being and takes note of your progress and readiness for change. During each session, you can count on your coach's full attention, active listening and supportive presence. Bear in mind that your progress is dependent on your personal commitment to the process. Your follow-up work between sessions and your commitment to the agreed actions are critical to your coaching success.

Wrap up Session

You arrive at the last session. This final session is purposely designed for you and your coach to take stock of the entire coaching process. This can include an overview of the benefits you gained, the learning you acquired, new behaviors you incorporated and your general level of satisfaction with the process. You will be invited to recall the key highlights of your coaching work, naming the sustainable changes and insights you gained, and the shifts in perspective that will enable your success and satisfaction now and in the future. While respecting your confidentiality, this session may include your organizational coaching sponsor (human resources or supervisor), if this was agreed at the outset.

Professional Coaching Agreement - example

Between Coach..and Client/Coachee...

The request or the context: ....

Objectives of the coaching program (generally 1 to 3)

1. Objective 1 ....

2. Objective 2...

Professional Coaching:

As a Client/Coachee, I understand and agree that I am fully responsible for my physical, mental and emotional well-being during my coaching sessions, including my choices and decisions. I am aware that I can choose to discontinue coaching at any time.

I understand that "coaching" is a Professional-Client relationship with my Coach that is designed to facilitate the development of personal, professional or business goals and to develop and carry out a plan for achieving those goals.

Methodology:

The coaching is carried out by Coach, according to the agreement, additional services may include: ....

Coachee may be encouraged and agrees to perform individual work between sessions, such as reading, personal reflections and defining/updating ongoing goals and action plans. For each session, both parties agree to be prepared to ensure maximum outcome.

Coach and Coachee agree to be respectful of each other's' time.

Cancellation conditions are the following: ....

The program consists of .... sessions with duration of .... hours /OR .... hours in total.

Coaching sessions take place in person at .... or by phone or Internet.

Confidentiality and Code of Ethics:

All coaching sessions are *confidential*, unless the coachee chooses to disclose the information.

Coach adheres to the .... code of ethics (for example, ICF Code of Ethics).

Terms and Conditions:

Financial conditions: ....

Client responsibilities: the client is responsible for his personal work, decisions and actions.

Coach responsibilities: the coach will give the means (time, skills) and is not responsible for the results.

Termination Conditions:

If the program is terminated at the request of Client/Coachee or Coach, remaining coaching hours may be transferred to another coachee, where applicable. No reimbursement is due. If the program is terminated due to the inability of Coach to complete the program, Client may choose between a suitable replacement of Coach or reimbursement of coaching sessions that have not taken place.

Date...

Signatures:

Client...Coach...

Manager or sponsor (if tripartite contract)...

AND NOW TO ORGANIZE YOUR AGENDA

When do we meet, where and for how long?

You can imagine the possibilities are endless. Coaches are very creative; they offer many options to clients. Each coaching mandate is "tailored-made" between you and your coach. Each coaching session is unique. Here we present some common and widely used logistics with our advice. In all cases, these details are discussed and specified in the agreement.

IV. Coaching logistics

Logistics	General details	Recommendations
Where?	Coach's office Coachee's office Meeting room Hotel lobby or other	A quiet and calm environment that allows for concentration and confidentiality.
How?	Face to face Phone call Videoconference Internet call	Both coach and coachee are fully available and free from interruptions. (Attempting a coaching session while driving is not a good idea!)
How long?	An average of 6 to 12 sessions, with possible extensions. Often executive coaching is 20 hours or more. Sessions can vary from 45 minutes to 2 hours or longer.	According to the objective, the duration of a coaching process varies from months to a year or more. The coach's objective is to ensure the client becomes autonomous.

WHAT HAPPENS DURING A SESSION?

Key moments of a coaching session

Each coaching session follows both the overall coaching objectives and specific focus for each session. The coaching conversation can be compared to a dance. Once music is selected, you and your coach must, like dance partners, establish a rhythm and coordinate your movements. If the structure of the conversation is initiated and guided by the coach, you are there to bring the content and solutions. In general, a session takes place in three main steps.

Opening

You arrive with a request, issue or situation that determines the focus of the meeting. Your coach again requests your full involvement to be present in the current moment. Most often, a connection is established between your current session's focus and your overall objective(s). You also share with your coach what you accomplished and what you meant to accomplish since your last meeting together with your assessment of the impact from your actions or inactions.

Heart of the coaching session

By this point in the process you have gained some insights and new perspectives. With this comes strengthened self-awareness and self-confidence, and you are in a safety zone where working at a more profound level is possible. Your coach encourages you to be authentic and mindfully aware. Your thinking and your perceptions deepen through powerful questions offered by your coach. Your coach may also propose a variety of exercises and practices, such as role plays, metaphors, or physical movements. Whatever the method used, the coach accompanies you in the present moment and explores with you where you want to go in the future. Together, you design and agree the way to get there.

Action plan and way forward

By now you have some new ideas about what comes next and it is time to take action. If this is not the case and you are not sure what action to take, your coach may take this moment to offer you his or her reflections and observations of what has transpired up to this point. Your coach ensures that you come away with a plan that suits you in terms of your current understanding, readiness to take a decision, and willingness to take next steps. Together you co-create a plan with specific actions and commitments to support your progress between now and your next session. In closing the session, your coach may invite you to connect your action plan to your main objectives.

COACHING REQUIRES MUTUAL RESPONSIBILITY

Coaching is a partnership where both parties remain mutually responsible. More and more research confirms the utmost importance of the relationship between you and your coach! At any point, if you think or feel that something is really not working for you, it is absolutely your right to suspend coaching or bring it to an end. This can be something as basic as your coach not showing up on time, not being prepared, not having your file on hand, not being available to schedule future sessions; or something more serious where the coach exhibits unacceptable behavior or makes inappropriate suggestions. This is one more reason to check the coaching agreement in detail before signing.

While this rarely occurs, if your coach does not comply with the ethics and standards of the profession, you can file a formal complaint with the professional association or federation to which the coach belongs. Diverse remedies are available depending on the seriousness of the offense, which may include imposing sanctions, ejection from the association or federation, or filing a lawsuit or other legal proceeding. As in any other profession, you might find "fake" coaches who are self-serving, unethical, greedy or otherwise demonstrating unprofessional behavior. The good news is that these categories of people who call themselves coaches don't last long as their reputations become known.

⟲ *What can I expect from coaching?*

After working with a coach, clients frequently confirm they gained more than they initially anticipated. As you can imagine, this "more" is unique to each client. Throughout the coaching process, your coach will guide you to take stock of where you are at various moments in time. At these intermediary reflection points, you have the possibility of realizing you have already gained deeper learning than you initially expected.

What new insights can I gain?

Insights: Throughout the coaching journey, you will gain awareness about yourself, your relationships, your immediate environment and the world at large. The approaches used by your coach help you discover your strengths, core personal values, "automatic pilot" thinking patterns, reactive behaviors, self-imposed limits and untapped resources. During this exploration, you may be struck by insights, revelations or new perspectives where suddenly things make sense. Whether during a session with your coach, or on your own, you may experience an "aha" moment where your eyes grow wide and you exclaim, "Oh, now I get it!"

What decisions are possible now?

Decision Making: Once you have identified options, your coach guides you to clarify and consider options carefully. This deepened reflection allows you to take decisions and commit to an action plan in which you agree to practice and observe between the current and next session. For example, read a specific book; ask for feedback from family, close friends or work colleagues; take mindful breaks to calm your mind and allow insights to arise; observe yourself practicing new behaviors, experience new places and meet new people. These actions are designed to help you learn more about both your decision making process and the decisions you take.

What new behaviors can I incorporate?

Changing Behaviors: Through regular practice and with the support of your coach, you progressively deepen your self-awareness and self-confidence, develop new thinking and incorporate new behaviors. This in turn generates renewed motivation, enhanced productivity and new ways of being. This work guides you to reach tangible results linked with your current objectives and also strengthens your ability and capacity to face tomorrow's challenges and to recognize opportunities.

⟲ *What about "unintended" consequences?*

Unexpected Events and Realizations. In addition to the outcomes you anticipated and achieved, unplanned or unexpected consequences may also occur. What do we mean by this? While positive outcomes could be that you learned to speak in public, you are more comfortable addressing conflicts with colleagues, or you are clear about your future steps, possible unexpected consequences could be that you discover you are not in the job that suits you, or that your new behavior at work changes the dynamics of relationships with your colleagues, or that you have more influence over your environment than you realized. A problem that seemed to be 100% your boss's "fault" turns out to be a mismatch of communication styles where a shift on your part brings positive changes in your relationship. In any event, both planned and unintended realizations bring to light new possibilities and perspectives.

⟲ *What if I feel dissatisfied with the process?*

Speaking Up. Sometimes during coaching, you may get the feeling that something does not suit you, or does not work the way you would like. You do not need to 'please' your coach. You are there to attain the goals you both agreed. It is your responsibility to tell your coach about your discomfort. This conversation is indispensable to reassess and adjust any issues, such as the coaching process itself, the manner and style of your coach, your expectations and your commitment to coaching. Be clear and authentic whatever circumstances arise. It will serve you well!

If you wait until the end of your coaching to express your dissatisfaction, you leave little room for anything more. The last session ends and you have no further coaching time. In such a situation, it is unlikely that either you or your coach will want to extend the relationship. So what happened?

The responsibility for this "crash" is shared throughout the process. Both of you missed the warning signals. However, even if your objective is not reached, we urge you to stay open to the possibility that something positive happened anyway. The long-term benefits of coaching are not always realized instantaneously. What was not obvious during the coaching, may well show up later. **Some clients say that several months or even years later they recognized how useful the coaching was.**

Our suggestions: throughout the coaching process, check your progress by asking yourself the following questions:

- ☐ Does my coach have the necessary tools, expertise and experience to help you reach my goals?
- ☐ Am I truly committed to the coaching process?
- ☐ Are my objectives and expectations suitable for coaching?
- ☐ Do I take the engagement seriously in terms of time and energy?
- ☐ Have I implemented the agreed actions? Completed my homework between sessions?
- ☐ On a scale of 1 to 10, what progress have I made toward my coaching objectives?
- ☐ Are my objectives realistic considering the allotted coaching time?
- ☐ Did I come for "tips and tricks" or deeper change?
- ☐ What do I really want from this coaching relationship?

Obviously, coaching is neither the solution for everyone nor the appropriate support for all circumstances. Sometimes people are not "coachable" or receptive to coaching; therefore coaching may not be the appropriate intervention. In other cases, it may simply not be the right time in their lives.

⌒ *Could I feel out of my 'comfort zone' during coaching?*

Dis-comfort Zone: Coaching often addresses deep change, the "level 2" change we mentioned earlier (see p.11). Profound change has the potential to touch and impact your way of living, to uncover your true identity, and to reveal your personal values and other important aspects of your life. Such discoveries can result in your feeling "destabilized" or out of your comfort zone. Like any transition, coaching may bring up moments of unease, questioning and doubt. Of course, as your coach guides you progressively toward your objectives, your new awareness and insights can produce shifts in perspective where you are now prepared to take major decisions. Any such changes can impact your personal and professional environment and relationships. Addressing deep change in coaching can bring up uncomfortable emotions in you and in those around you. It is highly advised to consider this broad impact before, during and after coaching.

As we know from research in psychology and extensive coaching practice, the path of major change can be considered like the grieving process. This process can manifest when you decide to abandon something *known* to commit to a future, yet *unknown*. None of us goes through this process with complete ease. Even when the change is desired, some discomfort is inherent in the process. At such points, the relationship of trust between you and your coach supports you and may give you courage Letting go of old habits and behaviors that no longer serve you, going beyond your limits, and opening to new perspectives can be highly beneficial. Moving through this period of discomfort is often what renews your enthusiasm, motivation and sense of purpose.

Our suggestions: At any point in the coaching process if you feel physically or emotionally tired:

- ☐ Tell your coach how you feel.
- ☐ Pay particular attention to your physical health, sleep and nutrition.
- ☐ Stay in touch with people who support you during the coaching process.
- ☐ Balance your efforts and treat yourself with lightness, care and compassion.
- ☐ Consider the benefits of the change you decided to make.
- ☐ Give yourself time, even a break from coaching, if necessary.

Throughout coaching, various realizations and insights as well as emotional upsets may occur. Your coach's role is to facilitate and support you through this process allowing you to recognize and release unhelpful ingrained habits and replace them with more productive behaviors. Moving out of your comfort zone is both challenging and rewarding.

In any situation, you absolutely retain your prerogative to say "no" when something does not suit you or makes you overly uncomfortable. By nature, any helping relationship deserves careful attention and agreement of boundaries concerning what is permissible and what is not. Manipulation, or abuse in any form, is absolutely not part of the practice of professional coaching. As we have previously advised, choose your coach carefully from a professional network that requires its members to adhere to a code of ethics. If the coach is a member of a coaching association or federation, you can register a complaint with the association for any breach of the code.

As you can see, the risks of engaging a true professional coach are quite small, especially when you take the recommended steps to ensure the safety and professionalism of the relationship. In all circumstances, the coaching process is designed to ensure that you retain your full decision-making power and autonomy.

Coaching is a deeply rewarding experience when you and your coach are aligned and agree on defined objectives and outcomes. The vast majority of clients are very satisfied with their overall coaching experience. (PwC, 2010)

Reasons for dissatisfaction pointed out by a number of organizations

- No clear specific goals were defined
- No evaluation and reporting system existed in the organization
- Choice of the coach was not validated by the coachee
- Individual being coached became too reliant on support of a coach and did not want to end the coaching mandate

Results from recent PwC survey (PwC, 2007)

LET'S 'LISTEN' TO A COACHING CONVERSATION

Here is a portion of a coaching conversation using the GROW model (see p.73). Coachee Anne's objective is life balance, and we start here:

 Coaching conversation using the GROW model

Anne is a senior executive in a multinational company headquartered in the US. She works long hours, is available at any time for conference calls regardless of time zone differences. She rarely takes vacation and checks her emails frequently even on evenings and weekends. She has no children and her partner also works a great deal and travels frequently for his work.

Anne - I love my job but I feel drained by the intense pace. I have no choice.

Coach - If you had a choice and you were not so drained, how would you like to feel?

Anne - I'd like to feel free and at the same time know that I have completed everything I need to do. (Goal - the goal)

Coach - When you do everything you need to do, how free do you feel on a scale from 1 to 10, where 1 is "I am not at all free" and 10 is "I am completely free"?

Anne – ah, no matter what I do, I never feel totally free. My response is 2 or 3 maximum, because I have always something else to do and it keeps turning in my head. (Reality - reality)

Coach - What have you tried so far to feel freer?

Anne – A couple of time I tried not to work at all - at least not during the weekends but my partner is also a workaholic. So, when I see him glued to his phone, I finally go back to mine. (Reality)

Coach - If I understand you correctly, if your companion were not working on the weekend, you could be free to enjoy your weekend?

Anne - Yes, absolutely! But it never happens! (Options)

Coach - What could you do to make it happen?

Anne - Maybe my partner Andrew would understand if I explained that it is important for me, and for us. We love each other a lot, but things have been like this for a very long time. Since our years at university, the two of us got used to working hard and taking no days off. Unfortunately, it is now our long-time habit.

Coach - When do you want to speak with him about the importance for you to take breaks?

Anne — Oh, I suppose I can do it today. I will pick him up at the airport during rush hour traffic so we will spend at least an hour or two in the car. (Options)

Coach — Great! This travel time will give you the opportunity to share with your partner that you really need to enjoy weekends without work. Is there anything else?

Anne - Yes, I guess I also need to get organized during the week, prioritizing my work to complete what is really urgent before the weekend. And Andrew will definitely have to do the same. (Options)

Coach — So you will speak with Andrew, get better organized at work, and invite him to do the same?

Anne — Yes, that sounds good. If we are talking about it openly and sincerely and if both of us agree on it, anything is possible. In any case, it now seems doable and I am excited for us to talk. (Wrap up - summary, conclusion)

Listen to a Senior Executive recount his impressive coaching success story.

As a demonstration of the power and impact of coaching **from the client's perspective**, you find here a recorded testimonial from a top executive who shares his experience following coaching with his executive coach.

For more >>
Listen to a senior executive client testimonial
www.professional-coaching.net

Timing and logistics of typical coaching engagements

Average length of coaching engagement:
- 47% between 4 to 6 months
- 26% between 7 to 12 months
- 18% less than 3 months
- 8% more than 12 months

Coaching engagements lasting 7 months or longer occur more frequently when clients are executives.

Logistics:
- 66% face to face (44% in North America; 85% in Europe)
- 27% telephone (50% in North America; 9% in Europe)
- 7% other mode of communication

Results from recent PwC survey (PwC, 2012)

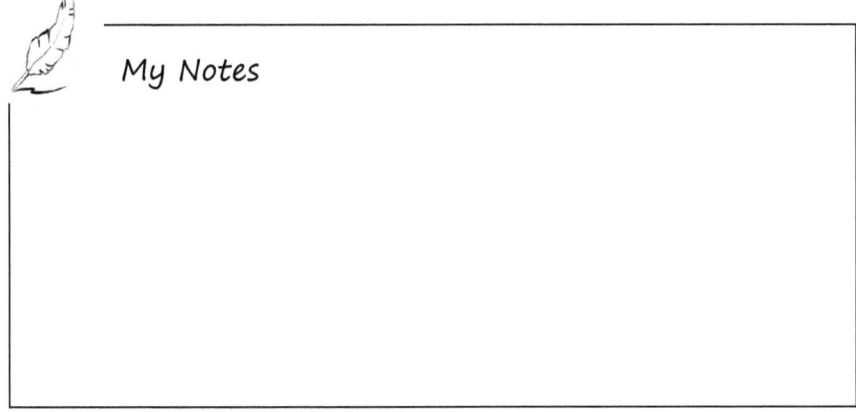

My Notes

SUMMARY
How Does Coaching Work?

✓ Objectives, methodology, timing, conditions are discussed and agreed in a signed written agreement.

✓ Coach and coachee are mutually responsible for the coaching process.

✓ As a coachee, it is your responsibility to speak with your coach if you are feeling dissatisfied or overly uncomfortable.

✓ Coaching success depends on your commitment to the entire process and to following through with practice between sessions.

✓ As a coachee you can expect, new insights, reflections, observations, taking decisions and making commitments, following an action plan, changing behaviors, and creating new habits and ways of being to serve you today and in the future.

The real voyage of discovery consists not in seeking new landscapes, but in having new eyes.

- Marcel Proust

6
WHAT'S IN MY COACH'S TOOLBOX?

The success of your coaching experience relies greatly on your coach's capacity to create a confidential safe space and a collaborative working relationship where you can learn, practice, develop greater self-awareness, and find your own solutions. To accomplish this, your coach is trained and experienced in specific coach competencies, uses a range of tools, techniques and models, and respects professional standards and code of ethics.

CORE COACH COMPETENCIES

The competencies and masteries associated with successful coaching are the subject of ongoing research and investigation. Through training, experience, supervision and practice, your coach has developed specific skills and competencies to accompany you to reach your goals and objectives in the best possible way. The top coaching associations globally have identified a highly consistent list of core coach competencies to accompany you through the successful coaching journey, many of which can be found online (ref to page with URLs).

As ICF credentialed coaches, we provide here the eleven core coaching competencies developed by the world's largest association, ICF. These competencies also support greater understanding about the skills and approaches used within today's coaching profession, and delineate the criteria for evaluation of the work of professional coaches.

These skills are recognized globally. Your coach must demonstrate proficiency in each of these skills throughout the coaching process. These eleven competencies are grouped into four clusters. They do not represent any kind of priority in that they are all core or critical for any competent coach to demonstrate. They set the benchmark for successful coaching.

ICF Core Competencies

A. Setting the Foundation

1. Meeting Ethical Guidelines and Professional Standards
Your coach must understand coaching ethics and standards and apply them appropriately in all coaching situations.

2. Establishing the Coaching Agreement
Your coach knows what is required in the specific coaching interaction and how to come to agreement with you about the coaching process and relationship.

B. Co-Creating the Relationship

3. Establishing Trust and Intimacy with the Client
Your coach creates a safe, supportive environment that produces ongoing mutual respect and trust.

4. Coaching Presence
Your coach is fully conscious and creates spontaneous relationship with you, employing a style that is open, flexible and confident.

C. Communicating Effectively

5. Active Listening
Your coach focuses completely on what you are saying, and are not saying, to understand the meaning of what is said in the context of your needs and wishes, and to support your self-expression.

6. Powerful Questioning
Your coach asks questions that reveal the information needed for maximum benefit to the coaching relationship.

7. Direct Communication
Your coach communicates effectively during coaching sessions, and uses language that has the greatest positive impact for you.

D. Facilitating Learning and Results

8. Creating Awareness
Your coach integrates and accurately includes multiple sources of information, and offers interpretations that help you to gain awareness and thereby achieve agreed-upon results.

9. Designing Actions
Your coach creates opportunities with you for ongoing learning and for taking new actions that will most effectively lead to achieving your agreed coaching results.

10. Planning and Goal Setting
Your coach develops and maintains an effective coaching plan with you.

11. Managing Progress and Accountability
Your coach maintains focus and attention on what is important for you, and leaves the responsibility with you to take action.

For more >>
ICF Core Competencies
www.professional-coaching.net

Additional Competencies for Executive and Business Coaches

For executive and business coaches who work in an organizational context, added skills and experience are recommended to ensure effective coaching interventions. Managing the overall coaching engagement can include other stakeholders, as an HR representative or manager. A sound understanding of leadership issues and knowledge of how to effectively partner with the organization are indispensable. Intercultural, organizational and team competencies are relevant. It is not unusual for clients to request the coach has prior expertise in their specific environments. Executive coaches often are former corporate executives with advanced degrees, and a large number of business coaches have previous working experience and understanding of the complexities and unique demands of organizations.

Commonly used Approaches and Tools

The relationship between you and your coach is essential to successful coaching. Who your coach is and what your coach does is highly important. Your coach must possess specific professional skills, and by integrating a wide assortment of coaching techniques and tools, your coach designs a full coaching tool kit. Coaching tools can be used during sessions or as homework between sessions and may engage key stakeholders.

Aside from the mandatory coaching skills training and client coaching hours, it is up to each coach to decide how to create a practical and professional practice. You may consider the coach "toolbox" a strange way to describe the tools, methods and approaches a coach uses to accompany and guide you, but this metaphor is often used to describe the wide variety of coaching techniques.

You will see in the following table some of the approaches and tools used by coaches.

V. Schools of thought, approaches and tools used in coaching (a non-exhaustive list)

Theories, subjects	Approaches	Tools
Psychology Sociology Neuroscience Systemic, systems Ontological and others	Humanist/client-centered Solution-focus Positive psychology Behavioral and cognitive strategies Appreciative Inquiry (AI) Somatic/holistic/integral Transactional Analysis (TA) Neuro-linguistic programming (NLP) Systemic constellation	Assessments and questionnaires 360° interviews Shadow coaching Role plays Metaphors Visualization Scales and evaluation wheels Questions Active listening Feedback

Let's meet some experts at the origin of coaching

Over the years, coaching has integrated a wide range of knowledge, research and practices from human sciences, philosophies and other theories. Psychology, sociology, philosophy, neuroscience and management theories are among the sources of inspiration for the science and practice of professional coaching.

Other sources include a large number of widely known experts with more specific approaches and we mention just a few here as examples: Carl Rogers – a prominent humanist psychologist and one of the founders of the client-centered approach; Abraham Maslow – another American humanist psychologist well-known for his concept of hierarchy of needs classification and peak experiences; Virginia Satir – psychotherapist known for developing a systemic experiential approach including the family constellation; Fritz Perls – a provocative psychiatrist who brought 'awareness in the present' moment to clients, which he termed Gestalt therapy.

As a coachee, you really do not need to understand the detailed background. If you are interested to know more about a particular practice, your coach can give you a basic explanation about the approach taken.

Most coaches use a combination of several approaches creating their own style and their unique toolset. This creativity is part of the richness of the art, science and practice of coaching. These come in various forms, and we name a small selection of some commonly used tools and techniques.

Assessments and psychometric tests

These evaluation methods are standardized and structured and can focus on personality profiles (e.g., MBTI), behavioral styles and preferences (e.g., DiSC), skills, emotional intelligence (e.g., EQ-i, MSCEIT), attitudes, beliefs, values (e.g., VIA), motivation (e.g., Hogan, FIRO B Element), leadership competencies and other attributes. Psychometric tests are reliable and valid.

Through specific training and/or certification, your coach has expertise in implementing one or more of these instruments. Often, these questionnaires or assessments are administered online and in many languages. A detailed report is produced based on your responses. Through a feedback session with your coach, you become aware of your key strengths and behaviors, untapped potential, and development areas to design and agree your action plan.

360° questionnaires or interviews

The 360° interview process is an often-used method to obtain confidential feedback and comments from supervisors, peers, direct reports and other key stakeholders. This important information is gathered from your stakeholders through multi-lingual online questionnaires or bilateral interviews conducted by your coach. Both collection methods are designed to offer you a wider perspective beyond your self perception. Your coach collates and prepares the feedback/feed forward session to discuss the findings with you.

This is one of the richest ways to gather information about the perceptions and impact you have on those around you. The 360° feedback report includes your key strengths, suggestions for further development as well as gaps in perceptions among your key stakeholders and yourself. A number of online assessments are in practice to reveal competencies and leadership characteristics (e.g., Hogan Assessment Systems, MRG Leadership Effectiveness Analysis).

Shadow coaching

Shadow coaching is a powerful tool to help you gain self-awareness and enhance your ability to recognize and adjust your behavior. In the role of "shadow coach," your coach observes you in a variety of work settings. This can include team meetings, presentations or other important business interactions. Your coach may observe body language, tone of voice and pace, style and manner of interacting and communicating, others' reactions, as well as time management and other daily habits. You benefit from immediate confidential feedback related to your specific coaching objectives.

Role plays

Role plays are designed to practice important and tricky situations in the confidentiality of your coaching session. This could be a job interview, presenting a proposal, or any other important conversation where you put yourself in the place of others. Do you have a dilemma with your boss, your partner, a client or customer? Roles plays offer you the possibility to explore the point of view from another person's position to gain new perspectives and create new possibilities.

Metaphors

The brain is a highly sophisticated neural network designed for prediction and analysis. It is as efficient as it is surprising. Sometimes, to find a solution to a problem, it may be beneficial to set aside the logical explanation and to tap into your imagination. Your coach may ask you: "In this situation, imagine you are someone or something other than yourself, what or whom would you be? And what would you do?" This is an example of a spontaneous response from a coachee: "I feel like a locomotive train moving at high speed on a collapsing bridge."

Visualization

Long used by athletes, visualization helps to imagine excellence in their sport. Business people use visualization to achieve success at work. Used in coaching, visualization helps you identify, imagine and realize your dreams and aspirations. These exercises can be journaling about already achieving a goal or your ideal life, or creating a vision board.

Self-measurement scales and life wheels

A measurement scale uses an imaginary cursor along a line with measures from "1 to 10" to help you visualize where you stand on a particular situation. A life wheel is a pie chart scale that helps you to name and better understand your roles in life and where you spend your time. Wheels can include both personal and professional roles, or be limited to one or the other. Using these tools before and after a coaching conversation helps you realize what progress you have made over time.

Personal values, beliefs, attitudes, obstacles, and resources

Much of the structure of coaching is designed to assist you to enhance and clarify awareness of your current situation, your current reality, and to provide the framework to imagine a more satisfying future. The exploration of your current state and what is most important to you is an essential starting point. What are your core personal values? What are your core beliefs – those that empower and those that limit your possibilities and perspectives? What resources do you possess? What has worked so far? What's holding you back? What are your key success factors? What are your unique strengths and talents? Your coach will guide and support you through this discovery process with a series of powerful questions and reflections.

Questions, active listening and feedback

Questions are one of the essential tools used throughout the coaching process and are a vital competence in any coach's toolbox. Your coach's ability to ask powerful, thought-provoking questions, to actively listen to your words and "behind the words," and to offer feedback enables highly effective coaching outcomes for you. **We put special emphasis on the important coach skill of asking powerful questions!**

GROW model

The GROW model is one of the best-known and most frequently used coaching models. (see case study p.61)

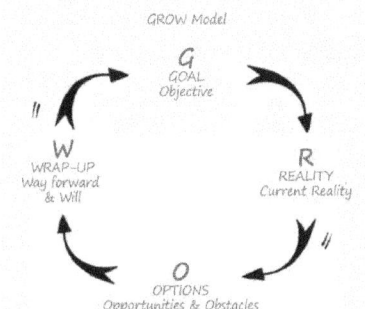

GROW Model

G
GOAL
Objective

W
WRAP–UP
Way forward
& Will

R
REALITY
Current Reality

O
OPTIONS
Opportunities & Obstacles

G = Goal: What is your goal or desired outcome? This element applies to each coaching session as well as long term.

R = Reality: What is your current situation, the current reality?

O = Options: What opportunities, possibilities and alternative strategies are possible? What obstacles stand in your way now or along the way?

W = Wrap up, Way Forward or Will: What is your plan? What will be done, when and by whom? What will (willingness) or motivation is present now?

The GROW process is presented sequentially here. In practice, it is a much less linear process which may start anywhere and revisit each of the stages several times. This model is an effective starting point and does not preclude the importance of other elements, such as the client's level of self-awareness, commitment and responsibility.

By no means is a complete list of all coaching tools and methodologies available and used by professional coaches. We chose some of the most common to provide you with an idea of the kinds of supports, exercises, assessments and models your coach might propose.

CODE OF ETHICS AND
PROFESSIONAL STANDARDS OF CONDUCT

Because it is a very important point, we would highlight it again: the coach who signs and adheres to a code of ethics and professional standards of conduct indicates a reliable sign of professionalism. It is rather like the Hippocratic Oath for doctors: it is a way to enforce what your coach can and cannot do. When your coach signs a code of ethics, this code may be included as an appendix to the coaching agreement.

The professional conduct of your coach is fundamental to the coaching process. We highly recommend you inquire of any potential coach what code of ethics they have signed. You can find the codes of ethics of other coaching associations on their websites. (see 136). Accepted by a growing number of coaching associations worldwide, U.S. law and the European Commission, ICF's thorough and extensive document covers a large number of points to define the code of ethics.

Below is a summary of some key commitments that all ICF Members worldwide agree and are obliged to uphold to remain members in good standing.

VI. Summary of ICF Code of Ethics

Section	As an ICF Member in good standing, your coach will:
Professional Conduct At Large	• Accurately identify coaching qualifications, expertise, experience, certifications and ICF Credentials. • At all times, strive to recognize personal issues that may impair, conflict, or interfere with coaching performance or the professional coaching. relationship and will seek professional advice if needed. • Maintain, store, and dispose of any records in a manner that promotes confidentiality, security, and privacy.
Conflicts of Interest	• Seek to avoid conflicts of interest and potential conflicts of interest and openly disclose any such conflicts. • Not knowingly take any personal, professional, or monetary advantage or benefit of the coach-client relationship, except by a form of compensation as agreed in the agreement or contract.
Professional Conduct with Clients	• Not give prospective clients or sponsors misleading or false information or advice. • Have and honor clear agreements or contracts with clients and sponsor(s) in the context of professional coaching relationships. • Be responsible for setting clear, appropriate, and culturally sensitive boundaries that govern any physical contact with clients or sponsors, and will not become sexually intimate with any current clients or sponsors. • Respect the client's right to terminate the coaching relationship at any point during the process, subject to the provisions of the agreement. • Suggest the client seek the services of other professionals when deemed necessary or appropriate.

Confidentiality / Privacy	• Maintain the strictest levels of confidentiality with all clients and sponsor information and have a clear agreement upon how coaching information will be exchanged among coach, client, and sponsor, and will not release information to any other person, unless required by law.

For more >>
the complete ICF Code of Ethics
www.professional-coaching.net

SUMMARY
WHAT'S IN MY COACH'S TOOLBOX?

✓ Professional skills, competencies and practices that are validated by a recognized coaching association or federation (e.g., ICF).

✓ Set of personal attributes and manner of behaving and communicating that suits you.

✓ Competence, chemistry and capacity to help you create greater self-awareness, identify strengths, uncover blind spots, remove obstacles, develop new capacities and ways of being.

✓ Recognized code of ethics and professional standards of conduct.

✓ Wide variety of validated and useful tools, assessments and practices to effectively accompany you on your coaching journey to maximize your full potential.

Happiness is not something ready-made.
It comes from your own actions.
- Dalai Lama XIV

7
WHAT DOES COACHING COST IN MONEY? TIME? ENERGY?

At this point of your reading, you no doubt realize that entering into coaching requires both your willful engagement and your personal investment. Like any important investment, it costs money, and also time and energy. To have a reasonable estimate from the start, we invite you to explore these points.

HOW MUCH DOES COACHING COST?

As in many other service industries, pricing regulation of coaching exists in few, if any, marketplaces; therefore the open market is the point of reference. The price of a session depends on the coach, coach's skills, experience, training, reputation, nature of the mandate, and it also depends on the coachee. Despite this jungle of variables, we still attempt to provide you with an answer other than "it depends" or is at the whim of the coach.

The question of coaching fees needs to be addressed before any coaching begins. Your coach's fees may be based on an overall program, per session, or per hour fee depending on the duration and purpose of the mandate. In addition, and we cannot say it often enough, a coaching agreement is a commercial contract like any other. As such, all the details of pricing, especially what is included in the fee, payment terms, cancellation conditions, travel policy and related expenses, or any other services should be communicated to you in writing and included in a legally binding agreement. This establishes a base of transparency and reliability.

Now you may be impatient to get to the heart of the matter: what fees do coaches charge? The average range is so wide that the price of a session may reasonably vary between $150 and $1,000 or more. While acquiring the necessary coaching hours for certification, some newly trained coaches offer very competitive rates or even pro bono in the beginning to gain actual experience working with clients. On the other hand, we know former top executives and leaders of industry and politics who combine consulting and "coaching" for astronomical sums. The aim of this book is not to take a stand on this topic, but to inform you of customary practices.

The reality of the market shows that life coaches charge lower rates (on average between $100 and $200) than those in the business environment (on average $250 to $1000+). These rates vary by region globally. Often the corporate, business or executive coach brings a wider range of experience, expertise and tools for which he or she has been trained and certified, and this may correspond to higher fees in recognition of the extent and depth of the engagement. In addition, more extensive preparation time is required of the coach to become familiar with the organization and culture, to review 360° or other assessment reports, and to prepare and participate in tripartite exchanges. The experience and reputation of the coach and also the nature and complexity of the issues entrusted to the coach have an impact on coaching fees. It is natural to consider a senior leader or key executive is "worth the investment!" And it is incumbent on the coach to honor this commitment.

Word-of-mouth references, reputation, location and logistics for coaching sessions, as well as the coach's level of expertise, training and supervision come into consideration with regard to fees. Where coaching is based on a combination of outcomes obtained and investment of time and energy on the part of the coachee and the coach, a program fee is more often quoted versus hourly fees. As stated before, these arrangements vary widely and are open for open dialogue and shared agreement.

Payment of coaching is by mutual agreement. All payment options may be considered: in full "up front" or in stages. This is in line with the practices of many other service providers.

 The legend of the broken-down cruise liner
(a coaching metaphor recounted by coaches)

The huge engines of a large cruise ship refused to restart. All the mechanics onboard attempted to fix it, but even after much time spent they failed. Then other expert mechanics were called in from far away. But still nothing happened; the engines remained silent. Then the captain remembers a man who had sailed for many years and is well known for his work on all kinds of engines. This man demands a tidy sum and requires payment in advance just to look at the ship's engine. The captain says he has no other alternatives so he decides to give him a try. When this highly anticipated man arrives onboard, he has only a small toolbox in hand. Everyone eyes him with raised eyebrows. He moves about among all the pipes and wires, bends, stretches, looks all around, remains silent, and then pauses thoughtfully. This takes some time, when suddenly he stops, pulls out a small hammer from his tool kit, taps sharply and quickly on a specific location. Immediately the purr of the engines returns. The captain is delighted that his ship can leave port and return to the sea. On top of this everyone now knows where and how to use a small hammer in case of problems. Thinking to himself, the captain is still quite puzzled, and truly surprised that such a small tap from a hammer can be both so expensive and highly effective.

Sharing with you this metaphorical story inspired by Eric Berne, founder of Transactional Analysis (Berne, 1964), we wish to illustrate that successfully achieving goals, whatever they are, cannot really be measured by a price. You are definitely the best positioned person to evaluate the balance between achieving your goals (needs) and making an investment (spending). Weighing the benefits of self-development, whether personal or professional, is not easily done with a spreadsheet but the return on investment is nonetheless worth considering pragmatically.

About Money

On this topic, we propose you ask yourself these questions:

- ☐ How do I consider the worth of realizing my desired future?
- ☐ What would boldness, courage and wisdom bring me?
- ☐ How much does low self-confidence cost?
- ☐ What is the value of a more effective way of working?
- ☐ What is the added value of strengthened self-esteem?
- ☐ What is the cost of not being promoted – or failing to ask for a promotion?
- ☐ What is the value of truly meaningful work?
- ☐ What does it cost to be stressed much of the time?
- ☐ At what price do I put on life balance? (family, work, play...)

- ☐ What could I gain by knowing my natural talents?
- ☐ What is the fair price of my dream come true?
- ☐ What is the cost of the status quo or of denying my need for change?
- ☐ If I do not engage a coach, what risks might I incur? What price could I pay in the long run?
- ☐ How much would new skills be worth?
- ☐ What can I gain by being happier? More resilient? More motivated?
- ☐ What do I really want that is worth considering hiring a professional coach?

You are better placed than anyone to know what budget to allocate to coaching as a unique gift to yourself, to your future self. If a coach is recommended by your company, it is an exceptional opportunity for you because it demonstrates that you are worth the investment.

What does coaching cost?

Average rates depend on:
- Characteristics of the coach
  - Coach within the company (internal coach)
  - External Coach
  - Number of years of coach's experience
  - Coach's expertise
- Type of the client
  - Private or individual clients
  - Organizations -varies on level: executives, managers, business owners
Fees vary widely in different regions around the world!

Overall average cost for all types of coaching: (PwC, 2009)
  - 50% of clients spent less than $2,094 USD
  - 50% of clients spent more than $2,094 USD

Results from recent PwC survey (PwC, 2012)

WHAT TIME IS NEEDED FOR COACHING?

Beyond the number of sessions, duration and frequency, we invite you to consider your time investment in the broad sense. Because we all know the pressure of time, we have all used the excuse of "lack of time."

Do you recognize yourself in any of these statements?

If I had more time, I would…

- ☐ Take better care of myself.
- ☐ Spend more time with those who matter most to me.
- ☐ Be able to solve this "problem."
- ☐ Think more effectively and make better decisions
- ☐ Be able to achieve my dreams and aspirations.
- ☐ Do what I really want to do!

Coaching is in fact this time you are seeking–time to focus on your priorities and what is most important to you! Concretely, engaging in coaching gives you a dedicated window of time with a professional outside of your day-to-day agenda and immediate obligations. With this time you are able to implement the learning gained through coaching and to realize sustainable results where it means the most to you.

Lasting change takes time and taking this time is essential. You've probably noticed how difficult it is to acquire a new habit even when you are totally convinced that it is good for you. To anchor a new behavior, to dislodge your outdated "automatic pilot" habit, and to feel comfortable with the new way of being requires time, practice and commitment.

Indeed, beyond the time with your coach, you are encouraged to set aside time for quiet reflection and journaling. Taking time on your own offers you another dimension for deepening your insights and learning. This time is not counted on the clock as time that "eats" into your leisure or sleep time. Rather, it is time you offer yourself to simply be in the present moment, to be an "external" observer of yourself. It is a time to observe without judging, to take note of your attitudes and behaviors as well as your personal and professional choices. Time spent engaged in coaching, with your coach and on your own, invites you to acknowledge your perceptions, emotions, thoughts in real time.

This time to acknowledge and calm your mind brings enormous benefits. Simply being aware of your breathing is a simple way to calm the flurry of thoughts and emotions. Taking even one minute as a regular practice brings a deeper awareness and presence of mind that serves you well in any situation. We all need to breathe – you are invited to simply pay attention to your breathe. Try it now. Witness the results for yourself.

At any point during coaching, if you struggle to find time to meet with your coach, or fail to complete agreed actions, your resistance to change is probably at work. This is mostly likely happening unconsciously. It is "time" to talk with your coach!

 Saving time rather than "losing" time

Through the restructuring, Jonathan, formerly a financial analyst in a bank, was appointed director of the commercial department with a team of fifteen people. To ensure his success following this promotion, Jonathan is offered a coach in order to strengthen his management and leadership competencies. For him, this is his first introduction to coaching and his first reaction was to imagine his agenda too full and that he had no time to lose with a coach.

Following a dialogue with the Human Resources Director and meeting with his proposed coach, he came to understand the importance of the first weeks in his new function and considered this opportunity to work with a professional coach as a high priority directly linked to his future success. As the coaching progressed, he gradually acquired the habit of reflecting before and after sessions, and to follow up on the agreed action plan most of the time.

Gradually, he was pleasantly surprised to see that he gained time rather than lost time. For example, simply take a few moments every morning to clarify his daily priorities and to review his accomplishments and unfinished projects at the end of the day saved him both time and reduced his stress level. He also started using train and air travel time, and even time in the elevator, to practice some stress reduction exercises. He even learned to take time for a walk outside to reinvigorate his energy level. In short, he incorporated what he learned in his coaching sessions and found himself better organized and with more time for more important strategic matters.

Some Tips for Managing your Coaching Time

- ☐ Planning sessions on a regular basis, for example, on the same day of the week
- ☐ Prioritize your coaching sessions
- ☐ Follow up on commitments between sessions
- ☐ Before each session, take time to prepare, reflect and plan
- ☐ After each session, take the time to collect your thoughts, feelings and insights
- ☐ Between sessions, consider how to apply learning from your coaching
- ☐ Take notes, keep a journal
- ☐ Use checklists to remind yourself of your commitments
- ☐ Dedicate the time necessary so that coaching is most beneficial
- ☐ If you believe you might be wasting time, talk with your coach
- ☐ If you run out of time, talk with your coach

AND NOW ABOUT ENERGY, WHAT IS NEEDED?

In addition to the investments in time and money, we have yet another essential element required for your success with coaching: it is your *energy*. As experienced coaches we want to remind you that any significant change requires an investment of energy: persistence, enthusiasm and resilience.

As confirmed by the most basic common sense, if the desired change implies modest behavioral shifts, medium intensity effort may be all that is needed. In contrast, where the intended change implies deeper modifications, more intense and sustainable energy is required. A major change requires abandoning what you are used to, so that you can discover what is unknown. Change often generates discomfort and resistance. At the heart of successful coaching, a period of disorientation, doubt or fear regarding the future may show up. Sometimes the temptation to abandon or to disengage fully is strong. To persist toward your objective, mobilizing your natural sources of energy is essential.

Wellness Energy is an important factor to consider before engaging in personal or professional coaching. During coaching, it is necessary to get adequate sleep, eat appropriately and lead a healthy lifestyle.

Energy of Patience and Persistence can also be valuable resources for achieving ambitious goals which take time and perseverance. Clients would like their coach to wave a magic wand to change everything instantly. But progressing step by step toward your goal is much more reliable and realistic, and in the end it is also more satisfying.

Energy of Courage is also highly useful. Indeed, it takes a healthy dose of courage to put yourself into question and to choose to evolve. You are well served to gather up your courage to meet and overcome the challenges and possible failures you may encounter along your "change" journey.

Personal and Professional Relationships Energy is also closely involved in the success of your coaching. In your personal sphere, sharing your progress and discoveries with one or two people close to you can support your coaching process and your ongoing evolution. For example, if your partner knows you as someone who arrives home overwhelmed and preoccupied by work, you may well create unintended worries if you suddenly begin asking what really matters in life. It is also desirable to share selected elements of your coaching experience with one or more of your trusted business colleagues. Benefiting from the support of a supervisor or another co-worker will increase your chances for success. Coaching is a process that honors you. There is no reason to keep it a secret. By learning to share, you can benefit from this invaluable source of energy and strengthened relationships.

What's the point of talking about your coaching experience with others?

After his second hospitalization for cardiac problems, Robert decided to "slow down." For thirty years, he devoted himself fully to the company he founded and up until now had prospered. He used to be everywhere at once, shouting and thundering at his staff and his suppliers. Given his recent health scare, he needs to calm down and at the same time ensure the smooth functioning of his company.

For this challenge, he hired a coach but kept it to himself. He decided not to share even with his wife or close associates. He felt that if he did, he would be accountable to them! However after a few weeks, Robert became discouraged. His wife kept telling him that he was behaving strangely and should consider changing his medication. As for his staff, they were speechless when he asked them "What do you propose to solve this problem?"

At this point, Robert almost gave up and was tempted to go back to his old ways. But when his coach asked him: "Ok, you have chosen to keep it secret, and you acknowledge it's a handicap. How does this serve you?" After long conversations with his coach, he finally decided to share with his team. Then they decided to expand the coaching mandate to include team coaching. His team members had to learn how to handle their responsibilities without Robert's intensive supervision. Both Robert and his management team wanted to work together to establish greater autonomy of his team. With his wife, tenderness and understanding definitely replaced her doubts and sarcasm.

So Robert discovered more than he expected by sharing with his family and team.

Taking into account the energy sources you need to support the coaching process, you become more aware of energy that comes naturally and is easily accessible. How does your energy show up? Are you curious? Are you persistent? Are you resilient? Are you bold? Are you creative? Throughout the journey with your coach, you discover many other resources which are useful to you not only during coaching but also in all aspects of life.

SUMMARY

WHAT DOES COACHING COST IN MONEY? TIME? ENERGY?

✓ **Money**: allocate a budget and consider it an investment that brings you both immediate and long-term value.

✓ **Time**: dedicate time regularly before, during and after your coaching sessions to ensure maximum benefit.

✓ **Energy**: identify your existing resources, those you need to acquire, and learn how to tap into your energy sources whenever you need them.

They didn't know it was impossible, so they did it.
- Mark Twain

8
HOW COULD MY EMPLOYER SUPPORT ME WITH COACHING?

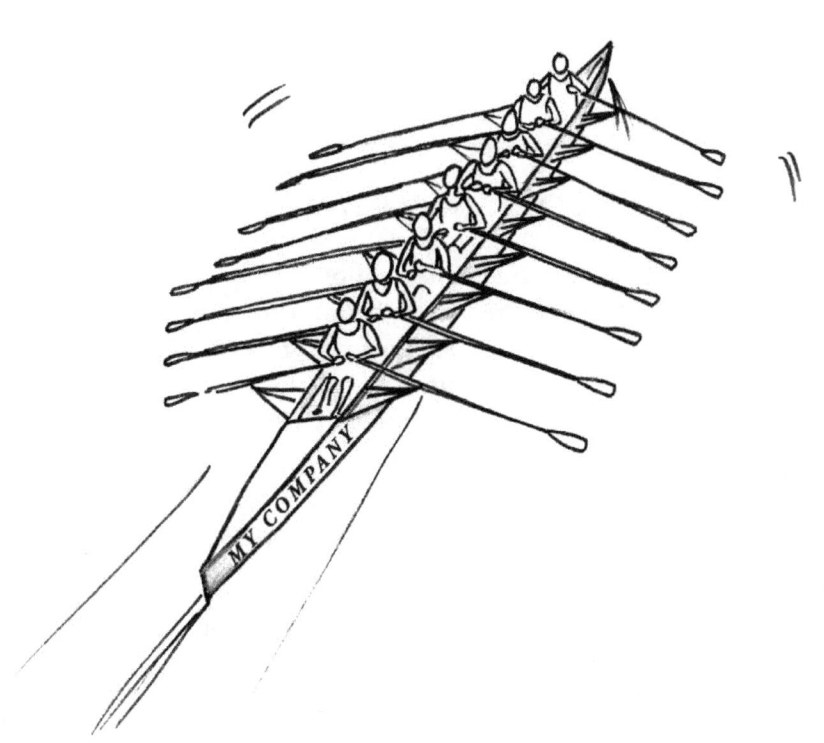

Coaching has evolved significantly over the past years. More and more companies and institutions are hiring professional coaches to support employees and to provide them the opportunity to grow and evolve.

Today in order to enhance employee engagement and improve performance, any organization is charged with delivering the means to develop its employees. This need is escalating. Talent management, life balance, stress reduction, effective communication are among the concerns facing organizations, regardless of size and complexity. Professional coaching effectively addresses all of these challenges in the present and for the future. If working with a coach simultaneously meets your needs and those of your employer, your request for coaching is likely to be approved. **Naturally, it is important that you are able to articulate clearly the benefits to your organization.**

WHERE DO YOU FIND COACHING IN ORGANIZATIONS?

First let's look at the most frequent situations where coaches are found in organizations. Perhaps you recognize below a situation similar to yours. Your employer is more likely to support your request when the objective promises mutual benefit. Obviously for private matters, such as family issues or personal relationships, your employer is not likely to grant your request for coaching.

VII. Typical coaching situations in organizations

For whom	Coaching Situations
Organization	• Defining the strategy and development of the organization through a system-wide coaching program • Ensuring the consistency across the organization, aligning with vision, mission, values and leadership attributes and competencies

Executive	• Raising self-awareness to open new perspectives and solutions • Focusing on core leadership competencies, achieving business goals, empowering and developing others, setting the vision and pace for success • Enhancing relational skills and navigating transformation • Increasing communication skills, self-confidence and executive presence
Manager	• Enhancing knowledge and management skills • Improving management style and versatility, decision making, delegation, communication skills • Raising awareness, resilience and motivation • Being effective in a new position or other transition
Team	• Creating a dynamic team, improving team working • Communicating more effectively for optimum performance, increasing creativity and responsiveness
All	• Balancing career and private life • Enhancing emotional, social and relational intelligence • Developing both personally and professionally

Coaching aims to enhance your competencies and performance at work, and at the same time, touches you more globally. It is obvious that when you develop personally, your employer also benefits. If you feel the need to hire a coach, it is always worth considering that your organization could support this endeavor. Before you reach into your own pocket to pay for coaching, keeping it a secret, we recommend the following steps:

- ☐ Get informed about the normal practices of your organization regarding coaching
- ☐ Identify the proper person(s) in your organization to support your request
- ☐ Know how to articulate your objective for mutual benefit
- ☐ Negotiate support concerning fees, time and/or other resources

What already exists in my company regarding coaching?

Some organizations currently have a coaching policy in place and offer this opportunity openly to employees. We even know some organizations that have designated budget and time for the same number of coaching hours for all managers. Much of the time the call for a coach is made discretely, in response to a specific need, and sometimes on the initiative of human resources or your manager. As mentioned above, it could be for someone who is struggling in a new environment, a newly promoted manager, a high potential employee, or someone who is moved to a new culture or country.

If you're fortunate enough to be in an organization already aware of the benefits of coaching, the process to request and engage a coach is already organized. According to usual business practices, you may be offered:

- an internal coach specifically dedicated to this function
- the opportunity to choose your own external coach (see p. 37)
- meeting with one or two external coaches from your organization's pre-selected coaching pool

Whom do I contact?

It is also possible that your employer has no previous experience with coaching. Take heart, there is a solution! With everything, we need pioneers who dare and you may well be one of them! In this case, the way you present and negotiate your request is crucial, because you must keep in mind that your employer becomes the 'client' who pays the coach.

For all such requests, it is important to contact the right person at the right moment with the right proposal. If at first you are not quite clear, you may want to find a trustworthy person at work to reflect with you so you are better prepared. In general, you should choose a person with whom you have an open relationship: your supervisor, another manager or someone from HR or training and development. Once this person is on board with your request, you have gained support to strengthen your request to a final decision maker, if there is one. This extra support may also come in handy during and after your coaching.

Now it is time to contact the person responsible for such decisions. If this person is unfamiliar with coaching, you have a chance to spark her or his curiosity about the benefits of coaching. Thanks to your initiative, your organization has the opportunity to become more familiar with professional coaching and its numerous benefits.

⌬ *How do I present my coaching request?*

Too often, people are reluctant to seek funding from their employer because they are afraid of bringing to light something that could be interpreted as a weakness. The temptation is very strong to keep any work issues or challenges private, especially in uncertain times. All too frequently our clients resist asking for support.

Obviously, you need to find a win-win solution, a sufficient reason for your organization to realize a return on investment. And this is the key word, coaching is an investment no simply a cost. So it is important that your coaching proposal includes a measurable return on investment. (see table ROI on coaching, p.102)

If your goal is clearly strategic and operational, be prepared to make a list of benefits that coaching brings and that your organization can verify. If your goal is more personal as in developing "soft" skills, such as enhancing your leadership competencies, managing stress, or improving life balance, your employer needs to understand how this personal development also will bring benefit to the organization. Your coach (or potential coach) may also assist you in the preparation and presentation. It is your responsibility to define specific measures and milestones to demonstrate the impact of coaching.

⌬ *What help could I request?*

Ideally, you receive approval for the complete cost of coaching, that is, the work hours needed for coaching, plus additional resources during or after the process. When this happens, you are clearly a valued employee and your organization cares for you and recognizes your contributions. Even if a full package is not granted, other possibilities exist.

As in any successful negotiation, whatever you obtain is better than nothing at all: partial funding, time during work hours, training, mentoring with a co-worker, etc. If you gain nothing else, you will have demonstrated your initiative and willingness to progress and find new solutions. In uncertain times, keeping a low profile might be tempting, but remember the capacities and skills gained working with your coach far outweigh the risk of making your request known.

Negotiating points to support your request for coaching

We invite you to imagine the advantages of asking your organization to support your coaching. No matter the outcome of your request, you could also be recognized for your readiness and capacity to

- ☐ Act with transparency and courage
- ☐ Demonstrate personal commitment and assertiveness
- ☐ Involve a supervisor and / or team in the process
- ☐ Integrate coaching into a professional development plan
- ☐ Demonstrate self-awareness and focus on personal, operational and strategic priorities
- ☐ Accept the challenge to improve professional competencies, relationship skills, and emotional intelligence.
- ☐ Integrate coaching tools to be a more effective team leader
- ☐ Expand leadership and communication skills.
- ☐ Raise curiosity for an innovative approach
- ☐ Introduce a new and proven approach to generate sustainable learning.

Consider that one or more of these outcomes may be sufficient to validate your request.

WHAT ABOUT TEAM COACHING?

The art of working together is both a challenge and a necessity in any organization. Those who succeed as a team vastly improve their capacity to innovate, achieve and sustain high levels of performance. Team coaching promotes collective intelligence as well as strengthening personal effectiveness and social skills. It helps to improve interpersonal relationships, communication, and team working practices, while considering the roles and responsibilities of each team member.

The role of a team coach is to provide the structure to facilitate dialogue and exchange, facilitate trust building, boost motivation, encourage creativity, stimulate learning and improve performance and efficacy.

Some examples of team coaching objectives

- Develop team cohesion and improve relationships to reduce conflicts and unnecessary pressure
- Define and establish best practices for remarkable performance
- Improve cross-functional coordination and breaking down silos
- Find innovative solutions to address team working and to challenge the status quo
- Learning to draw on the strengths of each team member for greater efficacy

How to respond if my employer offers me coaching?

From past experience, we know that coaching initiated by a supervisor or HR representative may not be well received. At best, this "imposed" coaching can be perceived as an unpleasant questioning of capacities, and at the worst as a serious warning. In fact, the message is twofold. First it indicates that you have something to change, and also that you deserve your employer's investment. If you consider the offer from this angle, you can feel honored and take this opportunity to fully engage in the proposed coaching and take full advantage of it.

Engaging fully in coaching allows you to:

- Validate your choice of coach, because a relationship of trust is essential. Even though coaching is proposed and sponsored by your organization, your agreement is important for your coaching to be successful.

- Express your objectives during the initial triad meeting to ensure that everyone agrees. You, your coach, your supervisor and/HR sponsor need a clear understanding and agreement on the coaching process, deliverables and outcomes.
- Verify the code of confidentiality. Each party must be clearly informed and agree on what is shared with the organization and what is not.
- Establish precise and concrete measures and timelines to document your progress.

Who pays for coaching?

On average, clients are almost equally split between those who pay for their own coaching (individual clients) and those for whom coaching is paid by a third party (sponsored clients).
 - Sponsored clients are more frequent in Western Europe (60%) and Oceania (56%)
 - Individual clients are in the majority in North America (55%)

The sponsored clients' share is significantly higher where the majority of clients occupy management positions within an organization.
 - 72% are executives
 - 69% are managers
 - 64% are staff members
 - 22% are business owners/entrepreneurs
 - 16% are individual/personal clients

Results from recent PwC survey (PwC, 2012)

Organization and employee mutually benefit from coaching

Vince is a senior manager in an import-export company. When he was promoted to head a team of fifteen people, his company offered him management training. Accepting this new challenge and at the same time experiencing some self-doubt, he took the initiative to hire a coach to help him gain more confidence. He made this choice on his own, decided to assume the fees personally, and to meet with the coach outside of working hours.

After a number of sessions, Vince realized that coaching allowed him to better implement the learning gained in the management training and to become visibly more effective in his function. The benefits of his coaching greatly benefited his company too. Sometime later, a restructuring merged his team with another and changed their job functions. To facilitate the blending of these two teams, Vincent proposed that his company hire a team coach.

Unfamiliar with this approach, his supervisor asked for detailed explanations about team coaching. Vince's request was granted and he was relieved to have the support of a professional coach through this delicate transition. This successful team coaching demonstrated to his management the tangible return on investment in terms of smooth team working, quick adaptation to the new structure while maintaining effective performance

SUMMARY

HOW COULD MY EMPLOYER SUPPORT ME WITH COACHING?

For your organization to support the coaching request, you can take the following steps:

- ✓ Verify usual business practices regarding coaching.
- ✓ Contact the person in charge of such requests.
- ✓ Define mutually beneficial objectives.
- ✓ Prepare and present your coaching request in a manner that is precise, clear and measurable.
- ✓ If necessary, negotiate for full or partial support.
- ✓ *Go for it! You have nothing to lose and everything to gain!*

The future belongs to those who believe in the beauty of their dreams.
- Eleanor Roosevelt

9
HOW DO I VALIDATE MY RETURN ON INVESTMENT?

The positive impact of coaching is now available to a much broader population and not only to the rich and famous, top champions, and senior leaders as it was before. Throughout our life from early education to retirement and, especially during active working years, everyone encounters situations where engaging a coach can be beneficial. Naturally, it makes sense to ask what valuable results you can receive from coaching.

How Can You Measure the Success of Coaching?

Depending on your personal situation, you can measure the return on your coaching expectations, around criteria noted in the table below.

VIII. Return on Investment: measuring your coaching results

Satisfaction and Motivation	What is your self-assessment? Are you satisfied? Do you feel motivated? Did you manage to achieve your agreed actions?
Learning New Skills	Did you learn new ways to progress at work or in your private life? Have you gained new skills, knowledge, competencies, behaviors and attitudes? How does your boss assess your progress?
Applying your Learning	How are you applying your insights and learning gained through coaching? What new habits, practices, behaviors and ways of thinking are you using now? How has your overall performance shifted?
Additional Insights	Besides achieving your specific objectives, what other advantages did you realize? What else is possible now? What about your dreams and grand ambitions?

The issue of measuring coaching benefits purely from a financial standpoint is sensitive yet interesting. What does it cost? What is the return? Some coaches work with their clients to help evaluate the monetary investment compared with the potential return. It is also very interesting to consider the cost of doing nothing! Some organizations are particularly attentive to this aspect and are interested to establish figures to support the return on investment related to coaching. Personally, nothing prevents you from attempting this calculation. However measuring the impact before and after coaching is not easy to quantify only using monetary terms. For example, how do you measure the impact of being happier, more satisfied, more confident and more motivated?

⟲ *How do I measure my financial and other benefits?*

- ☐ Staying in my current job
- ☐ Discovering my ideal career path
- ☐ Securing a desirable promotion
- ☐ More effectively managing my time and priorities
- ☐ Reducing stress
- ☐ Feeling more resilient
- ☐ Successfully moving through change
- ☐ Strengthening my communication and conflict resolution skills
- ☐ Deepening and enhancing my personal and professional relationships
- ☐ Feeling happy and enjoying peace of mind!

Customer satisfaction levels

- 83% of clients are very satisfied with overall coaching experience
- *92% of clients are very satisfied when the coach is an ICF Credentialed coach*
- 17% are somewhat satisfied

Results from recent PwC survey (PwC, 2010)

Return on Investment (ROI)

By design, not all types of coaching lead to monetary gains that are easily measured for the client (or their organization).

Personal coaching
- 67% of those who experienced a personal ROI indicated that they had at least a 100% return on their investment (ROI).
The median personal ROI indicates that those who seek a financial gain can expect a return in the range of 3.44 times their investment.

Business coaching
- 86% of those able to provide figures to calculate ROI indicated that their organization had at least a 100% return on their investment.

The ROI for organizations is quite a bit higher with a median return of 7 times the initial investment!

Results from recent PwC survey (PwC, 2009)

⨀ *How do I determine my specific list of benefits?*

Coaching is like a travel experience. You easily know if you arrived at the intended destination – or not. "I arrived" is a tangible result. However, it is more subtle to consider the benefits of the journey itself where you gain insights, consciously acknowledge and accept emotions, discover limiting beliefs and other intangible results. This set of results carries specific significance for each of us as individuals – and as employees.

Many organizations have already evaluated tangible and intangible results of coaching. We have gathered information from their surveys, studies and publications and share the following results. You can use these validated results to build your specific list of benefits.

IX. List of tangible and intangible benefits (a non-exhaustive list)

Tangible benefits measured objectively	Intangible benefits measured subjectively
• Achieved your agreed objectives • Increase personal and team productivity • Enhance your relational intelligence (employees, colleagues, clients, business partners, stakeholders) • Reduce stress and receive fewer complaints or work delays • Improve quality control, hence fewer errors, accidents • Improve overall performance: communication, negotiation, influence • Recognized for promotion and given more responsibility • Recognized executive presence	• Enhance self-awareness, self-confidence and self esteem • Develop flexibility, less judging and more accepting • Incorporate new habits and behaviors • Create more satisfying relationships, fewer conflicts • Gain new perspectives, improve decision making and strategic thinking • Attain a healthy life balance • Sustain good health and well being • Raise motivation, creativity, ability to respond • Gain greater clarity and insights • Generate positive atmosphere and sense of humor • Enjoy mindful living!

⟲ *What about unexpected discoveries or "bonuses"?*

You and your coach agreed specific objectives that are included in your written agreement. These are your explicit objectives. Even with this specific focus, you are likely to encounter more profound discoveries. Thanks to your coach's active listening and powerful questions, you are invited to reflect and open new perspectives. During the course of this introspection, you might realize a more in-depth objective to expand and deepen your initial objectives. For example, working with a coach, someone looking for a job may realize the need to strengthen self-confidence. This "bonus" objective or implicit objective is precisely the one that allows you to go further than you originally expected. This discovered "bonus" may affect you deeply and become a source of sustainable evolution and well-being.

Coaching Evaluation - example

Client name: .... Company name: ....

Coach name: .... Coaching period: ....

Objectives of the coaching program

1. ....

2. ....

A. Evaluation with regards to objectives

On a scale from 1 to 10 (1 = not achieved, 10 = 100% achieved), I evaluate the degree of progress in the achievement of my objectives

1. <u>Objective 1</u>

I started at: 1   2   3   4   5   6   7   8   9   10

I arrived at: 1   2   3   4   5   6   7   8   9   10

2. <u>Objective 2</u>

I started at: 1   2   3   4   5   6   7   8   9   10

I arrived at: 1   2   3   4   5   6   7   8   9   10

What helped me to make the progress? ....

What do I need to do to improve even more? ....

How am I going to use what I learned in the future? ....

B. General evaluation of the coaching process

1. How did I benefit from coaching, how did the coaching help improve my life/work?
....

2. What are the most important lessons I learned with the help of the coaching sessions?
....

3. What are the things I would not have done if I had not been working with my coach?
....

C. General evaluation of the coaching skills of the Coach

On a scale from 1 to 10 (1 = not satisfied, 10 = fully satisfied), I evaluate the degree of satisfaction

a. Empathy and understanding   1   2   3   4   5   6   7   8   9   10

b. Expertise   1   2   3   4   5   6   7   8   9   10

c. Setting challenges   1   2   3   4   5   6   7   8   9   10

d. Helping to generate creative
thinking and new perspectives   1   2   3   4   5   6   7   8   9   10

Comments/suggestions ....

Coachee - Date and signature: ....

WHAT IS THE ROLE OF YOUR COACH?

Serendipity can and often shows up in coaching engagements. With that said, we remind you once again that your coach is not a superhero; he or she has no more super powers than anyone else. From beginning to end, you are mutually responsible through each phase of the process. What happens depends on both you and your coach fully engaging in the thought-provoking and creative process to maximize your potential.

Your coach can serve you in a variety of roles. Depending on your coach's expertise and experience and your expectations and objectives, your coach may act as a:

- partner in your personal evolution
- facilitator of change
- catalyst for success
- resource to ignite your motivation
- developer of talent and potential
- explorer in the realm of possibilities

Let's face it, some coaches like to use such superlatives in their marketing messages. As with all such descriptions, use your intuition and experience to guide you to discover your coach's appropriate role as you build a creative working partnership based on trust and mutual respect. Coaching is a partnership of equals. As we have mentioned before, both you and your coach are in this important relationship together.

⟲ *What type of evaluation could my coach propose?*

In each session, your coach regularly solicits your feedback. How did you feel during the session? Is there something else before we close? What are you taking away today? Midway during the coaching process, your coach verifies your progress with you and uses this feedback to guide the following sessions. During or following the last session, your coach prompts you to evaluate the overall coaching experience as well as the effectiveness of your coach. Your coach may also request written feedback (often an online questionnaire or email) based on your objectives, the coaching process, and how you feel your coach supported you and your efforts.

Where business coaching is based on a tripartite agreement, the sponsor (supervisor or HR representative) may participate in the final session and provide feedback about observed changes in your behavior. In return, you may take this time to provide some benefits received which you are willing to speak about in the presence of the sponsor. We remind you that the coach is bound by confidentiality. Other than commenting on the coaching process itself, any feedback by the coach remains subject to your prior agreement and permission.

Whatever your initial objectives, the learning, insights and practices gained through coaching are likely to influence and modify your behaviors and mindset. People in your personal and professional spheres will probably notice changes in the way you behave and express yourself.

In a business environment, various psychometric assessments can be used to measure and benchmark before and after coaching. The 360° questionnaire is another method to collect observations from key stakeholders. This 360° assessment can take place at the midpoint or near the end of the coaching mandate.

Coachees often share with their coach the comments of those close to them at home and at work. It is not uncommon that the spouse or partner is the first to compliment the coachee for the positive shifts in their relationship.

When your coaching experience results in changes in you and your behavior:

- What will others notice?
- How will they experience and interpret the changes?
- What will they express to you? Or not express?
- What changes may oblige them to adapt?

As you can see, a wide variety of benefits can be attributed to the coaching process. We name a few here as examples and encourage you to stretch and imagine what you really want. Coaching is a powerful process with the potential to bring about remarkable shifts. The more you are willing to invest personally, the greater your overall return can be. The case study below – in the words of the coachee – demonstrates this point.

Senior Executive in a newly created role with a large multinational manufacturing corporation
(in the clients' words)

Initial Situation and Coaching Objectives: 1) My role was novel in that I was responsible to define and obtain approval for a completely new strategy for entry into a new market with a new business model. While the overall objective was clear, the process, tasks and organization to deliver it were unclear and subject to a high degree of uncertainty; 2) I had little contact with my manager (EVP) and so had limited input in terms of either guidance or feedback: and 3) My knowledge of the sector was limited.

Simply put, I was struggling. The objective of the coaching program was to reverse this condition and rebuild my self-confidence to empower me to trust my own judgment and to take more initiative in decision-making and gaining support from others.

Criteria for Success and Coach Selection: *The coaching was initially proposed by my HR Director who obtained the support of my manager for such an approach. I met with three very well qualified coaches. For me, the real differentiator was the sense of empathy from my chosen coach and how comfortable I felt with her even from that first meeting.*

Role of My Coach: *The most important attribute of the coach was the ability to engender trust since this allowed me to be completely open and honest. Beyond this the principal skills of the coach were insight based on high quality listening and the sensitivity to know when to press me further and when to take a more gentle approach.*

The methodology based on 15 sessions at 3-week intervals:
- Define and agree the objectives and name my personal values. These personal values became "anchor points" that ensured that we did not try to change anything which encroached on what I held most dear.

- Identify scenarios or situations at work that presented a need or opportunity to modify and practice new behaviors with my coach before taking it back on the job.
- We also reflected on key experiences of the previous period which was a key element in establishing the modified behavior as "normal."
- The final block of sessions was used to consolidate and internalize the learning gained throughout the process.
The description above of what was covered while correct is not complete. It makes it sound like a simple, logical, mechanical process whereas the reality is that it was a complex, emotional, non-rational journey. At times it felt very uncomfortable as I was pushing myself to do things or behave in a way that was not normal for me. The end result of the work I did with my coach is that I am more self-confident and decisive in what I say and do. I am better able to communicate and interact with others, particularly where there is misunderstanding, differing objectives or even conflict, in order to reach a solution. This is true both personally and professionally.
Finally the ultimate validation is that I was offered the job that I wanted two years ago but was turned down for not being "tough enough."

Evaluating impact of business and personal coaching

The mix of methods varies according to the coach's main specialty, the position of the client, years of coaching experience and geographical region
- 76% Client self-assessments
- 65% Documenting goals and benchmarking
- 61% Feedback interviews (35% in personal coaching)
- 44% Standardized assessment instruments (22% in personal coaching)
- 8% Other
- 4% None

Results from recent PwC survey (PwC, 2012)

SUMMARY

HOW DO I VALIDATE MY RETURN ON INVESTMENT?

✓ Establish specific and measurable objectives and review regularly with your coach as well as on your own.

✓ Identify any changes and evolutions - both tangible and intangible.

✓ Gather feedback from those close to you (personal and professional) on several defined points.

✓ Use the evaluation form to validate the benefits of your coaching experience.

We don't see things as they are,
we see them as we are.
- Anaïs Nin

10
COACHING IS OVER, NOW WHAT?

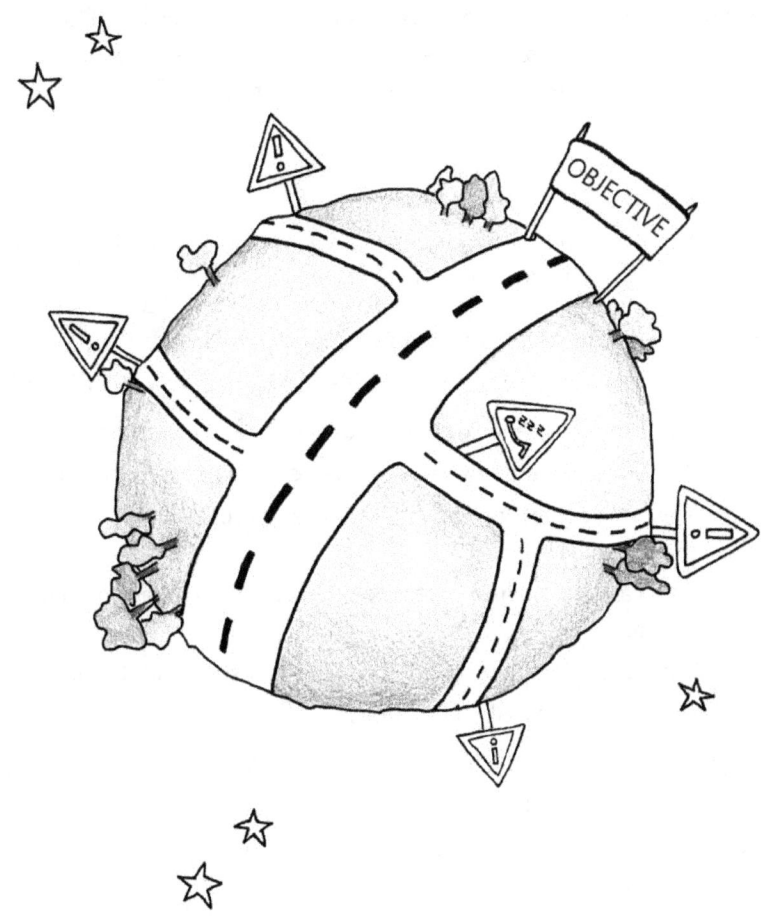

How do you maintain, develop and sustain what you learned through the coaching process? By now, you are probably aware that the results you gained through coaching are closely linked to your ability to pay attention and your capacity for change. With your professional coach, you were able to take time to reflect, explore new perspectives, and employ untapped resources to move forward. These new competencies are already serving you in a variety of situations, and will continue to in the future. Your coaching benefits will take hold and thrive more sustainability when you choose to put into action on a regular basis the best practices you have learned.

Determined intention is needed to sustain the benefits of coaching. Sharing our clients' experiences and our professional expertise, we wholeheartedly invite you to consider the following proven suggestions.

KEY REFLECTIONS FOR YOUR ONGOING JOURNEY

Common sense tells us that if you do nothing, new habits and other benefits may well dissipate over time. As you noted during your last coaching session, we encourage you to keep in mind your key priorities.

- ☐ What shifts in behavior have you learned and incorporated?
- ☐ What insights and new perspectives enable better decisions?
- ☐ How did you improve your personal and professional, relationships?
- ☐ How can you balance professional success with peace of mind and well-being?
- ☐ What coaching benefits do you want to sustain and develop?
- ☐ What will happen if you do nothing?

The following pages offer suggestions and practical ideas to deepen and sustain your coaching experience.

ENCOURAGE WHAT MATTERS MOST TO YOU

Coaching helped you develop new skills and competencies, gain insights, name your personal values, identify your unique strengths and incorporate new practices. Now that your coaching engagement is ending, the rigor and commitment to sustain these helpful practices becomes your responsibility. What can you do?

Perhaps when you entered the coaching engagement you were not aware of what was holding you back or not working as well as you would like. Continuing to make progress on the most important areas takes awareness and attention. It involves taking stock and making a commitment to take consistent, regular action.

Creating new habits takes time and practice!

Through your coaching experience, we deeply hope you learned to:

- ☐   Increase your self-confidence
- ☐   Strengthen your self-esteem
- ☐   Be more self-aware and mindful
- ☐   Set meaningful objectives and measure your evolution
- ☐   Discover your talents and embody your unique identity
- ☐   Nourish compassion for yourself and others

As you continue your positive evolution, you realize that what happens to you depends largely on the way you look at it and the stories you tell about it – the stories you tell yourself and others! You are mainly responsible for the way you interpret and respond to situations, feelings and emotions. Taking personal responsibility and holding yourself accountable allows you to adjust your perception of the world in order to create your path to happiness.

Welcome your unique genius by the way you show up in your daily life.

DEVELOP MINDFUL SELF-MANAGEMENT

By this point, you have completed a meaningful step with your coach. To get back to a metaphor mentioned earlier, the decision to continue the journey now belongs to you. Your coaching experience revealed you as a wiser and more attentive "traveler." During this time, you pushed beyond your limits and discovered new possibilities. Keeping this open-minded state of being, you are well prepared for a richer life journey.

Whether you encounter unpleasant or amazingly positive surprises along the way, your ability to remain curious, creative and compassionate helps diminish worries and opens avenues of opportunity previously unforeseen. Cultivating this wisdom sustains and deepens your coaching benefits.

How do I engage my "inner coach" to continue to seek understanding and hold myself accountable?

One of the major benefits of coaching is the structure, focus and guidance a coach brings to the process. As your own inner coach, you are well served to engage regularly in self-reflection. This practice helps you to be aware of your choices and to recognize the difference between automatic and optimal decisions and behaviors.

Whatever happens in the future, you are sure to experience unsettling situations as well as extraordinary opportunities. Your ability to be fully mindful in the present moment is an important practice that will equip you to cope with such challenges. Engaging your inner coach prepares you for dramatic developments, while helping you deal with the routines of daily life.

Self-development is an ongoing process. Consider this time an important priority and honor this commitment to yourself. Take care to dedicate resources to yourself – including time, energy and money.

What obstacles, limits and fears might I face and accept?

The challenges of life and the nature of our human condition remind us how vulnerable we all are. To recognize and name your true emotions takes wisdom. Acknowledging and accepting fears and limitations, while considering your own vulnerability with kindness and compassion is a daily challenge worth your effort. Paying attention to your bodily sensations (sight, hearing, taste, touch, smell) and becoming familiar with your emotional messages help you cope during periods of great turbulence. Whether you are on the road to success or facing potential failure, a clear understanding of your inner "gremlins" is essential to sustain your self-coaching practice.

INCORPORATE HELPFUL PRACTICES

As professional athletes know, the process of keeping fit and in shape is an ongoing commitment. The same holds true in the world of professional coaching. What is practiced becomes habit. While you are still in the rhythm of regular self-development, choose the practices that you find effective.

The challenge is to replace non-productive habits with empowering ones. We offer here some practical suggestions for your own Personal Action Plan. Choose and commit to several that appeal to you and feel free to add your own favorites.

How to define my future-oriented Personal Action Plan?

What to do	Why and how to take action
Make personal journaling a regular habit	One popular technique for documenting your learning journey is writing in a personal journal on a regular basis.
Cultivate self-awareness through meditation or other mindful practice	It has been proven that those who regularly practice meditation are more resilient, are more resourceful, make better decisions and are happier than non-meditators.
Find ways to relax and reduce stress	Yoga, Tai Chi, walking in Nature, swimming, listening to music, and other calming activities are essential to maintain well-being.

Dedicate time for self-reflection and identify learning resources	This is an excellent practice to carry your learning forward and to realize your full potential. A vast number of self-help books and online audio and video resources are available.
Meet new people and deepen your relationships	Your friends, work colleagues, social and virtual networks are rich sources of diverse opinions, fresh ideas and unexpected perspectives.
Develop your self-management skills	Your enhanced clarity and increased ability to focus enable better decision making, long-term success and peace of mind.
Seek and be open to feedback	Soliciting specific feedback is an excellent method to better understand the impact of your behaviors and how to improve.
Focus on priorities and manage your time accordingly	Defining and following up on your long-term goals and short-term activities is essential. Being comfortable saying "no" when needed helps keep you on track.
Define and live your life balance formula for sustainable well-being	Defining your priorities, designing specific action while paying attention to your core values and caring for your energy level helps maintain balance & well-being.
Share with others and identify role models	Sharing and modeling desired behavior is a valuable way to cultivate competencies, reinforce best practices and stimulate learning.
Create or use a personal reminder to recall your coaching experience	For example, keeping an image, quote, activity or physical object plainly visible throughout your day is an excellent reminder of your successful coaching journey.
Remember to enjoy your life journey	Laugh, hug a child, smell a rose, watch a sunset or sunrise, listen to music, eat chocolate, write a thank you note to a friend, do something light and playful.

Whatever you decide, allotting time for self-reflection, seeking feedback and feedforward, recognizing insights, planning your next steps, and taking action toward your goals help you reap even more sustainable benefits from your coaching experience.

STAYING FOCUSED ON YOUR OWN ISN'T SO EASY. WHAT ELSE CAN YOU DO?

⌕ *When is it time to reconnect with my coach or hire another coach?*

Some coaches offer a brief follow-up conversation after two or three months as a check-in and an opportunity to exchange congratulations. At this point some new ways of being, behaving and thinking have taken hold, and you have truly changed. Perhaps there are other areas where you are still not quite habituated to the new behaviors. A quick check-in with your coach could be just what you need. Or you have incorporated so much of your learning through coaching that this follow up exchange is a time to express the positive changes you have realized and enjoy a sense of achievement.

More and more executives and other professionals extend the initial coaching agreement with less frequent sessions to support learning and development over a longer term. Understandably, this phase is becoming more prevalent where creative approaches, adaptability and resilience are essential to successfully address rapid and frequent shifts.

In the future, you may reach a point where hiring a coach could again be useful. Whether you consider your previous coach or another coach, we encourage you to review the selection process to ensure the fit is appropriate for your current situation.

We wish you the very best as you continue on your personal journey of learning and development!

Top factors for which clients engage coaching services

- 41% Self-esteem / self-confidence
- 36% Work/life balance
- 28% Career opportunities
- 25% Business management
- 25% Relationships
- 24% Work performance
- 18% Interpersonal skills
- 18% Communication skills
- 18% Wellness
- 15% Team Effectiveness

96% indicated they would repeat the process given the same circumstances that prompted them to seek a coach in the first place.

Results from recent PwC survey (PwC, 2009)

My Personal Actions

1.

2.

3.

SUMMARY
COACHING IS OVER, NOW WHAT?

To sustain your momentum and continue your learning journey, we encourage you to:

- ✓ Stay focused on your short-term and long-term objectives, goals and dreams.
- ✓ Be clear about your core values and bring them to life.
- ✓ Practice regularly being mindfully present and aware.
- ✓ Take stock regularly, adjust and take action where needed.
- ✓ Call on your inner coach, a sparring partner, mentor or other support.
- ✓ Enjoy your journey!

Yesterday I was clever, so I wanted to change the world.
Today I am wise, so I am changing myself.
- Rumi

EPILOGUE

At this point you have a clearer understanding about professional coaching and what you can expect along your coaching journey. Being well informed about when and how to engage a coach is a positive starting point to ensure your success. Now, when you hear that little voice inside asking for help or inviting you to explore your potential, we hope you feel comfortable to hire a professional coach.

While this book is not specifically designed to illustrate in depth the art, science and practice of professional coaching, perhaps your curiosity about this burgeoning profession has been evoked. You find a multitude of excellent books and online publications to continue your discovery.

- **Art**. Coach and coachee enter into a dance of giving and receiving. This unique alchemy creates space for unlimited positive change.
- **Science**. Coaching is evidence based with roots in many scientific theories and philosophies. We have just scratched the surface with some helpful applications to provide you with living examples of when and how coaching can be useful to you.
- **Practice**. Coaching is a structured and validated practice. In this book, we provide you with firsthand knowledge and client testimonials of how coaching works. Much more remains to be discovered and shared.

As professional coaches, we are fully conscious that we are contributing members of a rigorous profession in ongoing evolution. Our commitment to continue to serve our clients with excellence is a key motivator to be active contributors and practitioners.

To those who are currently at optimal performance with plenty of resources, we wish you continued success.

To those who want to identify and engage your unique talents and untapped potential, and who are open to engage a coach, we wish you a successful coaching journey.

We strongly believe that through coaching for personal fulfillment or professional success or both, you can enjoy a happier, more satisfying and meaningful life that impacts the people around you and the world.

Happier people contribute to a better world.

CHECKING YOUR KNOWLEDGE: YOUR COACHING QUIZ

Now it's time to review what you have read and verify what you know about coaches and professional coaching.

1. *Where did the word "coach" originate?*
   a. From an elegant brand of luggage and bags.
   b. From a clever and gentle animal that lives in a labyrinth.
   c. From the Old French word "coche," as a stagecoach.

2. *Coaching works for those people…*
   a. who are very depressed.
   b. who intend to live on Mars.
   c. who are doing well and would like to attain specific objectives.

3. *The role of the coach is…*
   a. to give you advice.
   b. to make you do difficult and disagreeable things.
   c. to guide you where you want to go and help discover your unique set of talents and resources.

4. *Coaching professionals must…*
   a. buy their professional coaching card.
   b. be tall and strong.
   c. be specifically trained and certified by a globally recognized body.

5. *An effective coach can…*
   a. resolve all the problems you bring.
   b. decide what you need to do to feel better.
   c. enable you to find your own solutions.

6. *If your employer proposes a coach for you, you can...*
    a. vehemently refuse to accept and find a good excuse.
    b. say "yes" and really mean "no" and therefore do nothing.
    c. agree on a specific objective and commit to the coaching process.

7. *You know your coaching is effective when...*
    a. your coach calls you every day, including weekends.
    b. you can effectively resist even the smallest change.
    c. your coach is highly competent and you are fully engaged.

8. *The elements that enable you to choose a qualified coach are...*
    a. a freshly printed business card and a fancy website.
    b. very cheap coaching rates and offers you a teapot as a bonus.
    c. proof of coach-specific training, certification and membership in a recognized professional network or federation.

9. *What is professional coaching?*
    a. the latest fad.
    b. an opportunity to meet a super-hero in green socks.
    c. a way to enhance your self-awareness, to develop your potential.

10. *At the end of the coaching mandate, you...*
    a. are the richest and most famous person in the world.
    b. have eliminated all problems to the end of your life.
    c. have achieved your objectives and gained valuable skills.

(Answers on the following page)

Answers

If you chose "c" ten times, bravo, you got it!

All the responses "a" and "b" are false. If you chose any "a's" or "b's", we suggest you return to the question. ☺

If you do not change direction,
you may end up where you are heading.
- Lao Tzu

Coaching Words in Play.

Some of these words may inspire you to embark on your coaching journey. Feel free to add your own words.

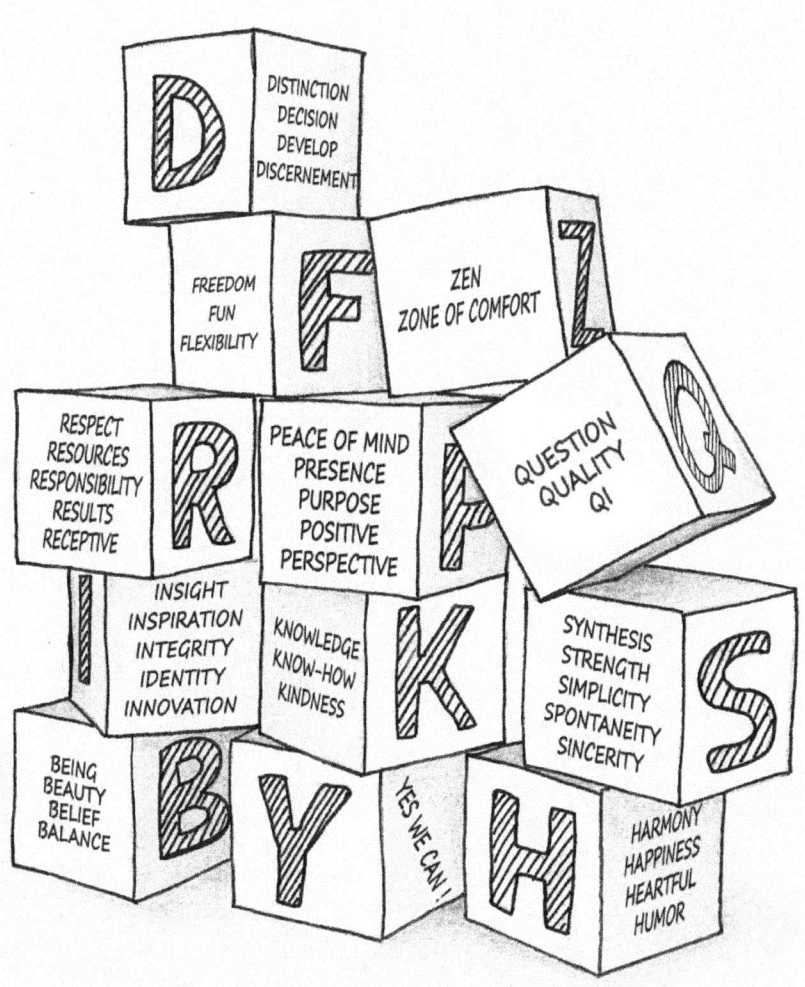

ACKNOWLEDGEMENTS

Dear Readers, first of all we want to thank you for reading our book and for your interest in coaching and professional coaches. Now that you have a clearer perception about our profession, you can confidently speak about coaching and back it up with validated information as well as experiential testimonials.

Thank you to our professional coach colleagues and to ICF for their rigorous endeavors to promote the art, practice and science of professional coaching. We are grateful for the investment in validated research and surveys that we cite in this book.

We thank our families, friends, colleagues, teachers, supervisors, mentors and clients who strongly encouraged us to follow our desire to explain more clearly and precisely about our profession so that a broader audience discovers that **coaching is an integral part of society**.

Warm thank you to Marion Depéry and Sophie Depéry, two talented designers, for the illustrations they have generously offered, and to Béatrice Tétaz for her IT support. – www.professional-coaching.net

Thank you to our reviewers and experienced coaching professionals, especially Leni Wildflower and Joe Treasure, who took time to share opinions and whose valuable and practical comments are included in this book.

Finally, we thank each other for the unwavering support we offered to each other while collaborating on this work, and especially for keeping our good humor, passion and rigor to explain and illustrate our profession. We hope you enjoy the book as much as we enjoyed writing and producing it.

ADDITIONAL RESOURCES

Suggested Reading

Tal Ben-Shahar, (2007) *Happier: Learn the Secrets to Daily Joy and Lasting Fulfillment*

Tal Ben-Shahar, (2009) *The Pursuit of Perfect: How to Stop Chasing Perfection and Start Living a Richer, Happier Life*

Rick Carson, (2003) *Taming Your Gremlin: A Surprisingly Simple Method for Getting Out of Your Own Way*

Stephen Gilligan and Robert Dilts, (2009) *The Hero's Journey: A Voyage of Self Discovery*

Rick Hanson & Richard Mendius, (2009) *Buddha's Brain: The Practical Neuroscience of Happiness, Love and Wisdom*

Jon Kabat-Zinn, (2011) *Mindfulness for Beginners: Reclaiming the Present Moment--and Your Life*

Fred Kofman, (ed. 2012) *Conscious Business: How to Build Value Through Values*

George Kohlrieser and Joe W. Forehand, (2006) *Hostage at the Table: How Leaders Can Overcome Conflict, Influence Others, and Raise Performance*

Max Landberg, (2009) *The Tao of Coaching: Boost Your Effectiveness at Work by Inspiring and Developing Those Around You*

Thich Nhat Hanh, (ed. 2008) *The Miracle of Mindfulness, An Introduction to the Practice of Meditation*

Matthieu Ricard, (2007) *Happiness: A Guide to Developing Life's Most Important Skill*

Philippe Rosinski, (2003) *Coaching Across Cultures: New Tools for Leveraging National, Corporate, and Professional Differences*

Martin E. P. Seligman, (2002) *Authentic Happiness: Using the New Positive Psychology to Realize your Potential for Lasting Fulfillment*

Peter M. Senge, (2006) *The Fifth Discipline: The Art & Practice of The Learning Organization*

Leni Wildflower and Diane Brennan, (2013) *The Handbook of Knowledge-Based Coaching: From Theory to Practice*

Note: some of these books are also available in eBook format

Authors' websites:

Françoise Depéry - www.deperypartner.ch
Nathalie Ducrot - www.prooptim.com
Virginia Williams, MBA - www.ventures-worldwide.com

Online bonus materials:

Professional Coaching! It is Time to Hire a Coach?
www.professional-coaching.net

- ☐ PwC survey and studies – Intro, p.3
- ☐ Conversation with a coaching expert – chap 1,p 11
- ☐ How Coaching Works – chap 2, p 25
- ☐ Senior executive coaching testimonial – chap 5, p.62
- ☐ ICF Core Competencies – chap 6, p 68,
- ☐ ICF Code of Ethics – chap 6, p 76

Members of the Global Coaching and Mentoring Alliance:

International Coach Federation –
  www.coachfederation.org (22,000 members*)
European Mentoring Coaching Council
  www.emccouncil.org (5000 members*)
Association for Coaching
  www.associationforcoaching.com (4000 members*)

*Membership numbers vary over time and are trending upward.

Works cited

Berne, E. (1964). *Games People Play: The Basic Handbook of Transactional Analysis.* Random House.

Hanh, T. N. (2008). *The Miracle of Mindfulness.* Rider Books.

Hanson, R. w. (2009). *Buddha's Brain: The Practical Neuroscience of Happiness, Love and Wisdom.* New Harbinger Publications.

ICF, E. &. (2011). *European Economic and Social Committee.* Retrieved from European Commission: http://www.eesc.europa.eu/self-and-coregulation/full.asp?w=n&ID=142

Kabat-Zinn, J. (2012). *Mindfulness for Beginners: Reclaiming the Present Moment - and Your Life.* Sounds True, Inc.

PwC. (2007). *ICF Global Coaching Study.* 5,415 respondents in 73 countries: PricewaterhouseCoopers.

PwC. (2009). *ICF Global Coaching Client Study.* 2,165 respondents in 64 countries: PricewaterhouseCoopers.

PwC. (2010). *ICF Global Consumer Awareness Study.* 15,000 respondents in 20 countries: PricewaterhouseCoopers.

PwC. (2012). *ICF Global Coaching Study.* 12,000 respondents in 117 countries: PricewaterhouseCoopers.

LIST OF TABLES

TABLE OF CONTENTS

ABOUT THE AUTHORS

Françoise Depéry, PCC, is passionate about people development.

 After more than 20 years in charge of Learning and Development in multinational companies, she helps managers and individuals in career transition to find their own way, discover their strengths and achieve personal and professional objectives. She is Chapter Leader for ICF Switzerland Suisse Romande. Bilingual French-English. www.deperypartner.ch

Nathalie Ducrot, PCC, as motivational coach, promotes the power

 of optimism, by enhancing relationships with oneself, others and the world. Passionate about motivation drivers and encouraging leadership, she recently published a workbook based on positive neuroscience to demonstrate motivation as an "inner process" of continuous learning. Her coaching practice combines recent insights in neuroscience, positive psychology and systemic theories. Convinced that our brain, mind and heart naturally have three powerful and reachable keys for Essential Motivation, her individual and team programs link one's unique identity, natural energy sources and inspired vision. Bilingual French-English. www.prooptim.com

Virginia Williams, MBA, PCC, is an executive coach, leadership

 and learning facilitator and former corporate executive. Optimistic and empowering yet realistic to the core, clients benefit from her strong global background leading teams, developing self-awareness, mindfulness and emotional intelligence, achieving sustainable results while respecting values-based strategies. Clients say her style is insightful, specific, confidence-building and catalytic. Her clients are multinationals, NGOs, business and team leaders. Creator of Executive Coaching programs: "Peaceful Productivity® - a Success Strategy to Unleash Motivation for Inspired Performance, Extraordinary Results and Peace of Mind." Bilingual English-French.

www.ventures-worldwide.com    @vworldwide